RAIL CENTRES:
SHEFFIELD

RAIL CENTRES:
SHEFFIELD

STEPHEN R. BATTY

LONDON

IAN ALLAN LTD

First published 1984

ISBN 0 7110 1366 7

Published by Ian Allan Ltd, Shepperton, Surrey;
and printed by Ian Allan Printing Ltd at their works
at Coombelands in Runnymede, England.

Title page left: **Approach to Victoria station,
29 November 1969.** *I. S. Carr*

Title page right: **The rare sight of a 'Britannia' on the
'Continental', Norwich MPD's No 70040** *Clive of India*
is ready to depart for Harwich on 30 May 1960.
J. F. Henton

Below: **Empty steel flatwagons are hauled up the
BR-built spur from Shepcote Lane to Tinsley yard by
Class 31 No 31.263.** *S. R. Batty*

Front cover, top: **Holbeck LMSR Compound 4-4-0 No
41068 awaits departure from Midland station with fish
empties for Wyre Dock on 5 October 1957.**
J. F. Henton

Front cover, bottom: **The 10.45 Manchester-
Cleethorpes at Sheffield, with a Class 08 shunter.**
S. R. Batty

Back cover, top: **'B7' No 61710 was one of the class
which did receive a BR number. Constructed in 1923,
the locomotive was built to the reduced LNER loading
gauge.** *P. Hughes*

Back cover, centre: **Class 37 No 37.102 plods uphill
with empty bulk containers past the site of Millhouses &
Ecclesall signalbox during September 1982.**
S. R. Batty

Back cover, bottom: **Last weeks at Rotherham (Central)
'Jubilee' 4-6-0 No 45593** *Kolhapur* **heads towards
Nottingham with a holiday relief train in the summer of
1966.** *L. A. Nixon*

Contents

Introduction and Acknowledgements

Sheffield's eminence as a producer of world-famous steel and cutlery perhaps would be expected to have produced the ideal conditions for the early development of a locomotive-powered railway system. It might be thought that the demand for raw materials, and the need for a reliable transport network to distribute the city's finished products, would have ensured the rapid establishment of railways in the town at the dawn of the railway age. Due mainly to geographical considerations, this did not take place. It was not until the second 'Railway Mania', in 1845, that Sheffield became firmly placed on the railway map, and more than a further half-century was to elapse before the city's railway connections were completed.

This book is my attempt to describe the growth of the main line railways of the area, including the more recent changes which have produced the railway system which exists today. I have not described the early wagonways, the detailed layouts of mines or steelworks, or the activities of the city's railway equipment manufacturers, as these subjects are outside the scope of the book and would indeed produce a vast quantity of material. Limitations of time and space are always present, thus the final text and the collection of illustrative material are the result of several sortings and selections.

Many people have provided help and assistance in compiling the story, notably the staff of the Sheffield Central Library Local Studies Department and the archivists of the National Railway Museum at York, especially John Edgington. Those who have contributed to the photographic content (either from their own work or from collections in their care) have eased considerably the burden of finding suitable material, as Sheffield was certainly an under-photographed railway centre prior to 1945. Valuable assistance was given by Ken Plant, Howard Turner and Dr Arthur Barnett, all of whom read the manuscript and offered constructive criticism. The final text is of my own choosing, and any errors must be laid at my door, not theirs! Howard's boundless enthusiasm for all railway matters of the area was a constant source of reference made freely available. Philip Robinson and David Pearce supplied many of the diagrams and much of the other illustrative material. To all these people I offer my grateful appreciation for their efforts. Last, but certainly not least, my thanks to Linda Bradshaw for her valiant work at the typewriter, and to my wife Andrea for her support during the many hours of research and writing.

Stephen R. Batty
Selby

Abbreviations

ECML	East Coast main line
ER	Eastern Region
GCR	Great Central Railway
GER	Great Eastern Railway
GGSJR	Great Grimsby & Sheffield Junction Railway
GNR	Great Northern Railway
GSCR	Gainsborough, Sheffield & Chesterfield Railway
GSWR	Glasgow & South Western Railway
GWR	Great Western Railway
HST	High Speed Train
L&B	London & Birmingham Railway
LDECR	Lancashire, Derbyshire & East Coast Railway
LMR	London Midland Region
LMSR	London, Midland & Scottish Railway
LNER	London & North Eastern Railway
LNWR	London & North Western Railway
LYR	Lancashire & Yorkshire Railway
MAS	multiple-aspect signalling
M&B	Manchester & Birmingham Railway
MGR	merry-go-round
MR	Midland Railway
MSLR	Manchester, Sheffield & Lincolnshire Railway
MSMJR	Manchester, Sheffield & Midland Junction Railway
NER	North Eastern Railway
NESW	Northeast-Southwest
NMR	North Midland Railway
PTE	Passenger Transport Executive
PW	permanent way
SA&MR	Sheffield, Ashton-under-Lyne & Manchester Railway
S&K	Swinton & Knottingley Railway
S&MR	Sheffield & Manchester Railway
S&R	Sheffield & Rotherham Railway
SCBAS&UJR	Sheffield, Chesterfield, Bakewell, Ashbourne, Stafford & Uttoxeter Junction Railway
SDR	Sheffield District Railway
SLJR	Sheffield & Lincolnshire Junction Railway
SMJR	Sheffield & Midland Junction Railway
SR	Southern Region
SYR	South Yorkshire Railway
WCML	West Coast main line
Y&NMR	York & North Midland Railway

Below: **A Harwich-Manchester (Victoria) draws into Sheffield (Midland) behind No 47.474 on 30 August 1974.** *Kevin Lane*

1 1813-1870 — Beginnings, Successes and Failures

In the early years of the 19th century Sheffield was linked by canals to Rotherham, Barnsley, Wakefield, Huddersfield, Ashton and Manchester. Although the importance of the city as a steelmaking centre was yet to be established, the industry had already been growing from humble beginnings in the later years of the previous century. The Sheffield industrialists had their eyes on the markets of Lancashire, and could see that a much better crossing of the Pennine barrier was essential for them to be able to realise their ambitions. As early as 1813 one William Chapman had proposed a combined railway/inclined plane/canal scheme to connect Sheffield via the Sheaf Valley with the newly-projected High Peak Canal, but the necessary $2\frac{3}{4}$-mile canal tunnel killed the idea. In 1824 a 'Grand Commercial Canal', from the Peak Forest Canal at Chapel Milton to Chesterfield (including a Sheffield branch), was proposed, and a further five schemes (varying in length and cost from 22 miles to $39\frac{1}{4}$ miles and £357,000 to £488,700) briefly appeared before the Cromford & High Peak Railway Act of 2 May 1825 finished off any future extension of canals in the area.

Later in the same year the Stockton & Darlington Railway proved the ability of steam locomotives for hauling goods traffic, and the industrialists picked up the challenge once again. Notable amongst the early campaigners was Henry Sanderson, a local land surveyor who disagreed with Stephenson's already well-known views favouring minimum grading of railway lines. Sanderson had the utmost confidence in the future of locomotive haulage, and in April 1826 he proposed a line from Sheffield's canal basin to the Peak Forest Canal at Chapel Milton. The line was to be 21 miles $7\frac{1}{2}$ furlongs in length, would need five inclined planes and stationary engines and two tunnels, and could be built for £150,000. Soon afterwards the Liverpool & Manchester Railway Act was passed and brought the benefits of locomotion a little nearer home, but still beyond the insurmountable Pennines. Matters slumbered until 1829, when the Rainhill Trials demonstrated

to the world just what could be done. The time for action had arrived, using locomotives instead of inclined planes and canals.

The railway history of the town involved many public meetings over the years, and the first one can be said to have been held at the Cutlers' Hall in the summer of 1830 to raise capital of £600,000 to build a Sheffield, Manchester & Liverpool railway under the supervision of George and Robert Stephenson. Strangely, despite their proven use of locomotives, the Stephensons wanted to use inclined planes and $6\frac{1}{2}$ miles of tunnelling along the formerly proposed route of a canal via Castleton. The ruling gradients would have been severe too — 1 in 99 westwards and 1 in 78 eastwards. Sanderson took issue with them and presented his own plans for a line which could be worked entirely by locomotives over a route via Penistone, Woodhead, Glossop and Stockport with respective gradients of 1 in 135 and 1 in 100. Much argument followed, but the company's provisional committee stuck by George Stephenson's plan for an eastward extension of the Liverpool & Manchester Railway to Chapel Milton via Stockport and Whaley Bridge. Accordingly, on 26 August 1830 the prospectus of the Sheffield & Manchester Railway Co was issued, naming Nicholas Robinson of Liverpool as Chairman and the Master Cutler, Philip Law, as one of three Deputy Chairmen. The other two were John Kennedy of Manchester and Charles Tayleur of Liverpool. Local committees were formed in each town, the Sheffield men being E. Barker, Joseph Read, John Rogers, Benjamin Sayle, John Shirley, J. Sanderson, W. Vickers, E. Vickers, Joseph Wilson, John Newbould, Charles Brownell and James Drabble. Financial matters were the responsibility of several small banks, including Parker, Shore & Co of Sheffield.

The possibility of a railway to Liverpool fired the imagination of the town, and on 4 September the *Sheffield & Rotherham Independent* published the following comments as part of an editorial item on the new project:

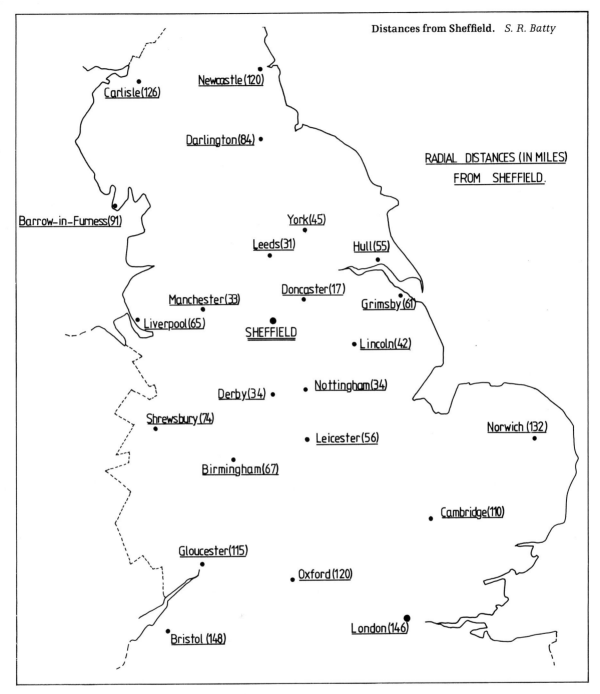

Distances from Sheffield. *S. R. Batty*

RADIAL DISTANCES (IN MILES) FROM SHEFFIELD.

Carlisle (126)
Newcastle (120)
Darlington (84)
Barrow-in-Furness (91)
York (45)
Leeds (31)
Hull (55)
Doncaster (17)
Manchester (33)
Grimsby (61)
Liverpool (65)
SHEFFIELD
Lincoln (42)
Derby (34)
Nottingham (34)
Shrewsbury (74)
Norwich (132)
Leicester (56)
Birmingham (67)
Cambridge (110)
Gloucester (115)
Oxford (120)
Bristol (148)
London (146)

'But to the town of Sheffield this project is one of almost incalculable interest and importance. Hitherto denied by circumstances, if not by locality, those means of improvement which canals have afforded to other manufactory towns, Sheffield has laboured under disadvantages which the perseverance and industry of its inhabitants could alone have surmounted.'

Strong stuff! After condemning existing roads and canals, and boxing the ears of the inhabitants for putting up with this state of affairs for so long, the Editor (Mr Robert Leader) then rounded on the establishment:

'It will hardly be believed that, at this time, they have no other direct means of conveyance for their goods to Manchester, than by carting them, either the whole distance, or about 23 miles, to the Peak Forest Canal, at a rate which the nature of the country renders very expensive: such, however is the fact — a fact which, in itself, constitutes a claim upon the country and the legislature which will certainly not be denied.'

But denial was to be the ultimate fate of the scheme. Stephenson described the means of ascending to Rushop Edge, using inclined planes and tunnels. Two planes would be used on each ascent, and trains of limestone (expected to be a very profitable commodity) would be used to counterbalance the ascending passenger trains. His description of the mechanics of the operation must have put the wind up many of the shareholders, with details of single-line inclined planes placed within tunnels with passing loops at the centre where, hopefully, passengers and lime-

stone would pass but *not* meet. Talk of passengers having braking control over the trains, and scotches being dragged along behind the last coach can hardly have been reassuring to the prospective railway travellers of 1831. That the Stephensons should propose and defend such a scheme after their successes with locomotive power seems incredible. George Dow has suggested that they regarded the S&MR as another mineral railway, rather like their Hetton colliery scheme of 1822, and also that demands upon their time were so great that they merely put their names to this particular plan. Whatever their successes and prestige amongst other early railway promotions, the reputation of the two Stephensons began to decline in Sheffield very rapidly.

The cost of the railway was estimated at £425,000 for a single line and £525,000 for double track. Henry Sanderson probed the plans again, and in September 1831 he publicly compared the actual cost of building the Liverpool &

Below: **Sheffield area map.**

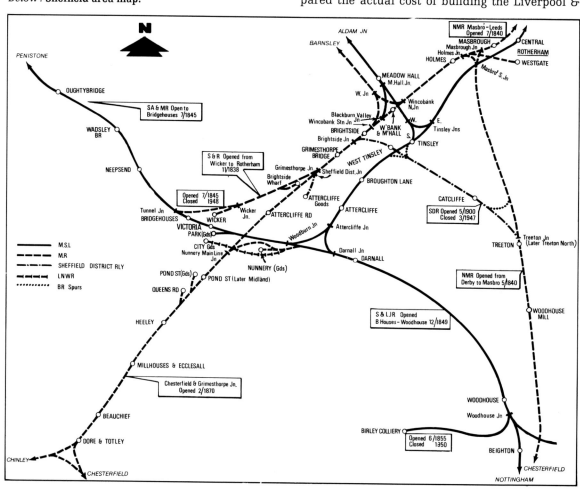

Manchester Railway with his estimated expenditure needed for the much more difficult proposals put forward by the S&MR. He tore Stephenson's estimate to shreds, showing that the much greater length of tunnelling needed, the number of bridges, river diversions, length of inclined planes and power required to operate them would add up to an expenditure of nearly £1million. Sanderson's arguments did not go unnoticed, for at the S&MR's first general meeting, in Manchester on 20 October 1831, the directors noted that the number of inclined planes had been reduced from four to two and the gradient had been eased from 1 in 18 to 1 in 36. Nevertheless, the assembly remained unhappy at the prospects and directed the provisional committee to consider further the practicalities of the entire project and to report to a special general meeting in six months' time. Nothing appears to have been settled, but the arguments went on and on. Matters came to a final head at the general meeting held in Manchester on 5 June 1833. Sanderson had been campaigning for his original route via Deepcar and Woodhead, and he stated quite confidently that the use of inclined planes could be avoided altogether by using locomotive power over his own route which involved a single two-mile tunnel. He completely destroyed Stephenson's estimated costs of tunnelling at Rushop Edge, and with all the estimates lying in ruins the entire railway promotion was abandoned.

Thus, whilst other pioneering schemes up and down the country were getting under way, Sheffield played no part in the nation's early railway development. But events moved quickly, and the slough of despondency was soon thrown off. The Liverpool & Manchester Railway was soon proving to be an enormous success, carrying far greater amounts of goods and numbers of passengers than had ever been hoped for. Its locomotives were reliable and they hauled well-filled trains. With inclined planes and canals now firmly pushed into the past, the manufacturers of Sheffield, Manchester, Ashton-under-Lyne and Stalybridge promoted another railway across the Pennines to unite all these places and be known as the Sheffield, Ashton-under-Lyne & Manchester Railway. Meetings were held in January 1836, the required capital was fixed at £800,000 and a provisional committee was appointed in May. This was chaired by Lord Wharncliffe and included the Master Cutler, John Spencer. Having had enough of Stephenson, they engaged Joseph Locke and Charles Vignoles to prepare separate surveys of the line, and both engineers presented their plans during October. Their routes were very similar (largely following Sanderson's proposals of 1833) and after resolving the slight variances the route was declared to go via Deepcar, Wortley, Woodhead and Dinting. In November the proposed capital was increased to £1million after the final scheme was settled upon. A three-mile tunnel would be needed at the line's summit, and the Sheffield terminus would be to the east of the (then) cattle market. Prophetically, Locke stated that the great reserves of coal to the east of the town would one day demand an extension of the line in that direction.

The scheme went before Parliament and passed through with little opposition and comparatively low preliminary expense on 5 May 1837. Thus the long awaited railway across the Pennines was at last under way, but several years of toil and trouble lay ahead of the SA&MR before the line was completed. Meanwhile, Sheffield's first railway to open to the public was already well under construction, with its terminus at Wicker, not too far away from the SA&MR's proposed alignment. This was the Sheffield & Rotherham Railway, a very short line born out of George Stephenson's routeing of the North Midland Railway through Masbrough, Rotherham. If the 'Father of Railways' was ever in any doubt regarding his unpopularity amongst the people of Sheffield after the S&MR fiasco, then their reaction to his plan for the North Midland Railway to bypass the town altogether can only have confirmed his worst suspicions. In passing from Derby to Leeds via Ambergate, Clay Cross, Chesterfield, Staveley, Eckington, Masbrough and Normanton, the towns of Sheffield, Barnsley and Wakefield were avoided in order to maintain a ruling gradient of 1 in 130. Appropriate branch lines from these places were to connect with his main line, but this was seen as simply not good enough for Sheffield. Charles Vignoles thought that the NMR could be brought into the town, and the mighty George Hudson tried to talk Stephenson into it, but both failed.

A public meeting was held at the Cutlers' Hall in January 1836 to examine the NMR route, and a Mr Leather of Leeds was appointed to survey a direct route to Chesterfield. To cover the cost a subscription was set up, but the poor response led to accusations of tradespeople's apathy. Leather's survey was discussed at a further meeting in March, at which it was decided that his route did not offer a practical alternative to Stephenson's branch line suggestion. Dissatisfied with this, the merchants and tradesmen resolved to fight the NMR and support Leather on their own account, and immediately raised £690 for the cause. Leather proposed a route from Rugby to Leeds via Leicester, Alfreton, Chesterfield, Sheffield, Rotherham and Royston, totalling 106 miles compared to the 126 miles of the North Midland's route from Rugby. Argument raged locally, and the NMR protagonists backed Stephenson's proposals at a meeting in the town hall on 30 May, stating that Leather's route was '... bringing the North Midland through Sheffield across that Hilly District to the South and South-East, forming as it would a series of lofty and dangerous embankments.'

The NMR supporters had not been idle. Forming the Sheffield, Masbrough & Rotherham Railway Co, they then surveyed a route along the Don Valley through Brightside and Meadow Hall to a junction with the proposed North Midland Railway at Masbrough (via a spur from Holmes) and on to a terminus in Rotherham known in later years as Westgate. Not quite everyone was completely happy with the idea — the upright citizens of Rotherham feared the dreadful consequences of allowing the 'drunken and dissolute' portion of Sheffield's population to have improved access to their town. Both the North Midland and Sheffield & Rotherham Railway Bills went before Parliament together, and both received the Royal Assent on 4 July 1836. Meanwhile, Mr Leather and his supporters fought on with their own alternative railway scheme. As a last, desperate attempt Leather joined with Joseph Locke in proposing a Sheffield & Midland Junction Railway in June 1836. This was to run from the terminus of the proposed Manchester line in Sheffield (the SA&MR was finally being proposed in a practical form at this time) to a junction with the Midland Counties Railway along the Trent Valley. The estimated capital was £900,000, but the NMR Bill going through Parliament streamrollered the idea. This was the first attempt of several to gain a direct southbound exit from the city, and nearly 35 years were to elapse before this cherished dream became reality.

The first general meeting of the Sheffield & Rotherham Railway Co was held at noon on 9 August 1836 in Sheffield Town Hall. Capital of £90,000 was to be raised by issuing 1,000 £25 shares and by borrowing as authorised by the Act. William Ibbotson was appointed Chairman, Henry Walker Treasurer and Thomas Badger and Henry Vickers as clerks. In October the company tendered for earthworks and civil engineering contracts, and advertised the post of secretary at a salary of £150pa. This position was filled by Thomas Pearson, who kept a diary of events leading up to the line's opening. He noted that work on the line started (apparently without any ceremony) in 'John Shepherd's garden at Brightside' on 27 January 1837. The company's Consulting Engineer was Isaac Dodds, owner of the Holmes engine works near Masbrough. He and

Below: **Holmes station on the original Sheffield & Rotherham Railway, looking towards Rotherham in early BR days. Some of the original buildings can be seen on the left.** *D. Thompson*

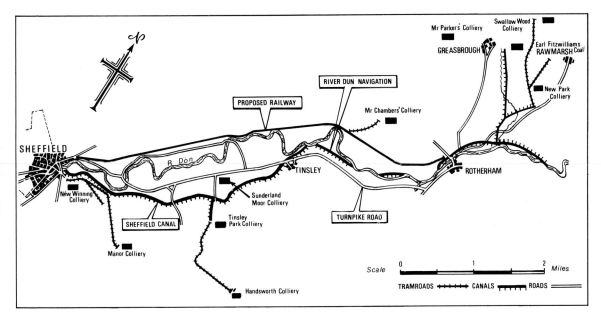

Above: **Map of proposed Sheffield & Rotherham Railway, 1835.**

Pearson produced a design for a locomotive turntable, which was built at the works and installed at the Wicker terminus. Quality of workmanship must have been a cause for concern, because Pearson noted on 15 October 1838 that the turntable was being installed for the third time. Some second class passenger coaches had been received, and he commented 'putty v. soft, and has run about the windows.'

In July 1837 tenders were invited for supplying wrought iron rails in maximum quantities of 1,000 tons, and also for chairs, keys and spikes. The first locomotives were delivered in August 1838, when *Victory*, *London* and *Leeds* were purchased from Robert Stephenson and *Agilis* from Murray, Fenton & Jackson of Leeds. (Another locomotive, *Rotherham*, was delivered in 1839 from the Leeds firm of Bingley's. This was probably one of two locomotives tendered for which had to be capable of hauling 100 ton gross at 20mph and be delivered by 30 November 1839.) The checking and preparation of locomotives was witnessed by Pearson, who wrote of 'steaming No 183 in the Engine House', cleaning out cylinders and 'finding swarf in the springs due to lack of oil.' The S&R must have been anxious to finish the line and start earning some hard cash, for a public service was advertised as starting from 1 November 1838, despite the fact that only one track had been laid two weeks before this date, and the earthworks had a decidedly unfinished appearance. Departures from Wicker were to be at 08.00, 09.00, 10.00, 12.00, 14.00, 16.00 and 18.00 (plus one at 19.00 on Mondays), and from Rotherham at 08.30, 09.30, 10.30, 14.30, 16.30 and 18.30. The fares were one shilling (5p) first class, ninepence ($3\frac{1}{2}$p) second and sixpence ($2\frac{1}{2}$p) third class. No tips were to be given, and smoking on the station was not allowed.

The days leading up to the opening produced great excitement in the area, and led to no mean amount of trouble for the townspeople. Pearson noted on 10 and 11 October that the English and Irish were 'fighting on the line' and 'Harding going to Barracks for Soldiers with Mr Hy. Walker's order for that purpose.' The resulting clash with authority did not completely dampen the navvies' spirits, for the next day Pearson tells us 'The Artillery going again to Rotherham, and the town in a state of alarm. Lord Fitzwilliam there, 30 rioters apprehended at the Court House. The line was officially opened on 31 October, and the first train conveyed Earl Fitzwilliam and several guests along the line to Rotherham, where they arrived at 11.00. A celebration breakfast, followed by the usual speeches, was held at the Court House. The three Stephenson locomotives were in use, and the return to Sheffield was used to convey there the Rotherham proprietors and invited members of the public. Next day came the public opening, and at Wicker a large area was roped off for spectators, and policemen and railway employees were issued with wooden staves with which to keep the peace. The first

Above: **A BR special leaves Masbrough and approaches Holmes behind Class 37 No 37.037 on 7 October 1978.** *G. W. Morrison*

Below: **From Grimesthorpe Junction the original S&R line today serves the steelworks of Firth Brown. This view shows the line heading towards Grimesthorpe, from just outside the original Wicker station site.** *S. R. Batty*

train was drawn by *Victory* and consisted of 300 passengers crammed into six black and yellow carriages. The short journey of just over five miles encountered 14 bridges (with more being built) and traversed embankments up to 18ft high and cuttings up to 41ft deep. No tunnelling had been necessary, and no intermediate stations had yet been built. The first such station was provided at Grimesthorpe Bridge, but this disappeared from the timetables in January 1843. *Victory* steamed to Rotherham in 17min and every lineside building, tree and vantage point was fully employed by the crowds who had turned out to witness the event. *London* followed 2min later, and the two return trains departed 15min apart. The first return train passed *Leeds*, on an outward journey, near Meadow Hall.

The S&R opened in splendid isolation, being no more than a short branch line until the NMR could be constructed through to Leeds and Derby. Coal traffic was carried from 7 August 1839, when a branch was opened from Holmes to the Greasbrough Canal, enabling coal from Earl Fitzwilliam's wagonways to be carried directly to Sheffield without using canals. The facilities at Greasbrough were rather primitive, and were scheduled for improvement during 1840 when it was felt that these were responsible for poor results on the coal traffic operation. At a shareholders' meeting on 15 February 1840 details of arrangements for working after the North Midland opened later in the year were discussed. A great improvement in traffic was hoped for, and a depot and booking office were being built at Wicker to cater for the increased traffic. Despite its short length and poor local trade, the S&R had managed a small profit over the year and a dividend of 15 shillings was paid per share. A slight drop in the number of passengers carried during January 1840 (26,809 compared to 27,941 in the previous year) was accounted for by a large reduction in the number of Sunday journeys made, as vociferous opposition to such a sacrilegious practice as travel on the sabbath had been made made by many clerics and their congregations.

To simplify working arrangements with the NMR a decision was taken in April to allow NMR stock to work throughout from its main line into Sheffield. This would avoid train-changing on reversal at Masbrough. Offices and works were to

Below: **The peace of Christmas Eve 1975 is shattered at Brightside as an unidentified Class 46 accelerates through the station on a Newcastle express.**
L. A. Nixon

Above: **Class 45 No 45.069 passes Masbrough Station South Junction with the 07.40 Cardiff-Newcastle on 21 September 1976. The lines in the foreground are the NMR Leeds-Derby route, and the original S&R line to the Rotherham terminus passed to the rear of the signalbox.** *B. Morrison*

be built at Wicker, and managed by a station committee. The division of receipts and expenditure would be based on the amount of traffic generated along S&R and NMR lines. By early 1840 the North Midland works were running at a fast pace, with 4,500 men working on six miles of the route near Beighton. The eight-arch viaduct here was finished after only five months of work, and the opening of the NMR main line was fixed for 11 May 1840. Services to Derby, Birmingham and London were timetabled as follows:

London-Sheffield down/up services						
London (Euston Square)	dep	06.00	09.00	13.00	20.30	
Derby	arr	12.45	15.00	19.45	05.40	
Sheffield	arr	15.15	17.30	22.15	08.00	
Sheffield	dep	05.30	09.15	12.00	14.00	18.00
Derby	dep	08.00	11.45	14.30	16.30	20.30
London (Euston Square)	arr	15.30	18.30	21.30	23.30	05.30
Sheffield-Birmingham/Birmingham-Sheffield						
Sheffield	dep	05.30	09.15	12.00	14.00	18.00
Derby	dep	08.00	11.45	14.30	16.30	20.30
Birmingham	arr	10.15	13.45	16.30	18.45	22.45
Birmingham	dep	03.15	06.45	10.45	13.00	17.30
Derby	arr	05.40	09.00	12.45	15.00	19.45
Sheffield	arr	08.00	11.30	15.15	17.30	22.15

The S&R timetable was suitably altered to provide good connections. NMR fares from Derby to Sheffield were 11s (55p) first class and 7s (35p) second class, whilst the S&R reduced its second class fare to 6d (2½p) and dispensed with third class travel altogether. The great day arrived, unfortunately with typical English summer weather to dampen the spirits. The North Midland metals were actually laid as far north as Oakenshaw, and Hudson's York & North Midland Railway had been completed as far as Burton Salmon on its way to Normanton. At 05.30 the first train carrying through carriages for Derby left Wicker station, but due to the 'newness of the engines and wetness of the weather' a total of 65min was lost on the journey to Chesterfield. The first down train arrived in Sheffield just before noon. Despite poor timekeeping and miserable weather, the events of the day produced great excitement. Before much longer the NMR line would be completed to Leeds and the Y&NMR would reach Normanton, so improving beyond measure the communications between Sheffield and the North of England.

Through journeys to London involved travelling over the Midland Counties Railway and the London & Birmingham Railway, and this facility was inaugurated in a more curious and entrepreneurial manner than the Derby service. W. Vickers, the S&R Chairman, sent the belt-driven locomotive *Sheffield* with one coach on the entire through journey. Departure took place on Monday the 11th and arrival was expected sometime on Wednesday the 13th! Mr and Mrs Vickers were the only passengers to Derby, but from there they were joined by George Stephenson and Michael Longridge, producer of the first wrought iron railway lines. An element of farce crept into the proceedings when the L&B promptly fined the S&R the sum of £10 for running over the L&B without first having given the necessary 14 days' notice!

At the end of May the North Midland announced expectation of completion through to Leeds on 18 June, but this was quickly revised to 1 July. A through London-Sheffield mail train was advertised to run from 11 June with a morning and evening service, but this working was delayed until 23 August when an evening train only from the capital was put on. Meanwhile the NMR station at Beighton was completed, and a timetable was published on 27 June for a London-Derby-Sheffield-Leeds-York-Hull service. Travel to York and Hull was possible due to simultaneous completion of the Y&NMR to Normanton and of the complete Hull and Selby Railway.

Below: **Class 31 Nos 31.250 and 31.270 head northwards past Masbrough Station North Junction with a Locomotive Club of Great Britain railtour on 21 April 1979. The lefthand tracks lead on to the ex-NMR 'Old Road' to Chesterfield, whilst those on the right curve round to Holmes and Sheffield along the former S&R route.** *J. S. Whiteley*

Hull-London up weekday service

Hull	dep				07.30	11.00		17.15
York	dep	06.15	07.30	09.00	12.30			18.45
Leeds	dep	06.45	08.00	09.30	13.00		16.30*	19.15
Sheffield	dep	08.00	09.15	10.45	14.15		18.00	20.30
Derby	dep	10.45	12.00	13.10	16.45		20.30	23.00
London	arr	18.00	18.45	19.00				05.30

*The 'Western Mail' continued to Birmingham.

Sunday service

Hull	dep				17.15
York	dep	07.45			18.45
Leeds	dep	08.15	13.30	16.30	19.15
Sheffield	dep	09.30	14.45	18.00	20.30
Derby	dep	12.15	17.00	20.30	23.00
London	arr	19.30			05.30

London-Hull down weekday service

London	dep				06.00	09.30	13.00	20.30
Derby	dep	05.55*	09.30	12.45	15.30	20.00	03.15
Sheffield	arr	08.00	11.45	14.45	17.30	22.15	05.15
Leeds	arr	09.15	13.00	16.00	18.45	23.30	06.30
York	arr			16.30	19.15	24.00	07.00
Hull	arr			18.00	20.45		08.30

Sunday service

London	dep		08.00		20.30
Derby	dep	05.55*	15.00	19.00	03.15
Sheffield	arr	08.00	17.15	21.15	05.15
Leeds	arr	09.15	18.30	22.30	06.30
York	arr		19.00		07.00
Hull	arr				08.30

*The 'Western Mail'.

Prior to the official opening, privileged persons had been allowed to inspect the line. The West Riding Geological Society had made the trip from Leeds to Derby during the two weeks up to 1 July and was presumably impressed by the civil engineering works along the way. For the great day itself, the intention was for the first NMR train from Leeds to meet and couple up with the S&R train from Sheffield at Masbrough, and then travel on to Derby. A small party left Wicker at 09.30 and arrived at Masbrough at 09.45, only to find no sign of the Leeds train. This latter had in fact departed at 08.00, but unspecified difficulties delayed their progress. Rain was falling again and the Sheffield passengers could only gaze at the engine water pumps and pre-heating boilers as they perhaps daydreamed of a direct line to Chesterfield, regardless of Stephenson's gradient philosophy. Eventually the Leeds train arrived at 10.30, with two locomotives leading and one bringing up the rear. After some smart operating the S&R portion was attached and the lengthy train departed. Unfortunately the engines steamed poorly, and this, together with wet rails, led to further time being lost on the climb to Clay Cross. Derby was reached at 13,15, where the (by now) ravenous passengers quickly detrained and grabbed a cold lunch before returning at 14.30.

Left: **A Sheffield-Leeds DMU stops at Rotherham (Masbrough) No 1 platform, 28 August 1982.** *S. R. Batty*

Above: **York '9F' 2-10-0 No 92206 hurries south along the NMR main line near Beighton with an express freight.** *L. A. Nixon*

Popular railway travel for citizens of Sheffield arrived on Monday 28 September 1840, when a half-price excursion to Leeds was run by the NMR. The summer of 1840 must have been a pretty miserable affair, as wet and cold weather once again prevailed. Nevertheless, the trip was fully booked upon departure at 10.00, when no fewer than 61 carriages departed between five locomotives for Masbrough. No wonder the route was lined by thousands of spectators! At Masbrough yet more carriages and a further locomotive were attached before departure for Leeds, which was reached at 12.30 amidst cheers and congratulations from a waiting crowd. The return train left at 20.30, but the task was too great and shortage of steam delayed the arrival at Wicker until 01.00. Despite this the excursion was deemed a great success and such trips became common events at holiday times.

Until 1841 the S&R made a reasonable profit, with a healthy income being derived from the mail trains (which had settled down to a steady service of one up and one down train daily by September 1840) and fresh traffic from the recently-opened Manchester & Leeds Railway via Normanton. Unfortunately, matters deteriorated quickly from August 1841, when operating costs increased beyond the revenue being taken. Several economies were made, including the decision not to proceed with a suggested branch line to exploit the coalfields around Swinton and Wath-on-Dearne, so leaving these available for the MSLR/GCR and Hull & Barnsley Railway over the next 50 years. During 1842 the Midlands and North of England became gripped by stagnation and depression. The NMR appointed a committee

to examine the future prospects, if any, of the company. One man on this committee seized the opportunity to further his railway aims — George Hudson. The committee's report called for more economies, which the shareholders would not accept, and all the directors except Hudson resigned. Both the Birmingham & Derby Junction Railway and the Midland Counties Railway were verging on collapse, and Hudson sought to amalgamate these with the NMR (which, in practical terms, included the S&R) to create one grand railway.

By February 1844 the S&R had decided that expansion regardless of cost was the only way to protect itself. A start was made by deciding to go ahead as quickly as possible with a short connecting line from Wicker through to the SA&MR line at Bridgehouses, which by this time was well under way. No expenditure was deemed necessary at Wicker, where up to five times the present amount of traffic could be handled. The half-yearly meeting of August 1844 was a messy affair, with no agenda, list of proprietors or financial results being provided. There was even confusion as to the exact date on which the meeting was supposed to be held. After bitter complaints about the loss of value of the company's shares, and even some allegations of dubious share trafficking, a very grim picture of the state of the railway was painted. The locomotives were almost worn out, and trains often had to be cancelled because of no power being available. Bad management was at the root of all the problems, and even the chairman agreed that

Above left: **The Wicker station end of the tunnel to Bridgehouses, seen in May 1952. An early example of cut-and-cover work, much relining work had to be done over the years. This view clearly shows the reduced bore diameter.** *Dr A. L. Barnett*

Above: **The SA&MR end of the tunnel in early BR days.** *P. C. H. Robinson*

Above right: **A large garage now occupies the site of Wicker station, but the blocked-up entrance to Spital Hill Tunnel and its surrounding masonry remind the observer of the area's railway origins from the 1840s.** *S. R. Batty*

Right: **Woodhouse Junction controls access between the former MSLR and MR main lines via the short spur through Beighton. A pair of Class 20 locomotives approach along the former MSLR line from Sheffield and prepare to cross over towards Beighton PW depot in January 1983.** *S. R. Batty*

the state of the railway left a great deal to be desired.

By 1843 the recession was fading quickly, and money for speculation became available again. Hudson's Great Midland Amalgamation Bill went to Parliament and was passed successfully on 10 May 1844, so creating what was to become the mighty Midland Railway. During September the S&R began negotiations with the Midland for either sale or lease of its railway to the new giant. Terms were quickly signed and the Midland agreed to work the line from 10 October. The little S&R existed on paper until the takeover was

finally completed by an Act of 21 July 1845, which ended the line's separate existence and sacked all its directors.

Across the town near Wicker, the Sheffield, Ashton-under-Lyne & Manchester Railway had spent several exciting and eventful years since the final scheme had gone before Parliament. Just after the railway was first proposed, and well before it went for its Bill, two schemes were announced to use the terminus for starting new lines to the south. In July 1836 the Sheffield & Midland Junction Railway was begging £900,000 capital to build southwards and meet the Midland Counties Railway at Nottingham. The idea sank into oblivion, but the second scheme did not die so

easily. In October 1836 the SA&MR committee met at the Cutlers' Hall to discuss extending its planned railway southwards. Four routes were considered: (1) as per the failed SMJR to Nottingham; (2) via Renishaw and Hardwick to the NMR at Clay Cross; (3) to join the NMR at Woodhouse Mill; and (4) as 3 but using a tunnel to reduce the gradient. The third option was chosen, the first scheme being thought unlikely to get through Parliament, the second being too steep and the last as being unnecessarily expensive. A prospectus was issued in November 1838 calling for capital of £150,000 and naming Hugh Parker as Chairman, Leather as Engineer and Lord Wharncliffe as principal advisor. The route was declared as being from the SA&MR station near the cattle market to the NMR at Woodhouse Mill via the 'townships of Attercliffe-cum-Darnall, Tinsley, Catcliffe, Orgreave, Handsworth or Handsworth Woodhouse, Aston with Aughton.' The scheme came to nothing, but had turned heads towards a direct exit southwards from the town and had laid the foundations of any extensions eastwards to Lincolnshire.

Soon after receiving its Act in 1837 the SA&MR had to make economies. Several doubting Thomases believed that the line's costs had been grossly underestimated, and consequently the Sheffield terminus was brought westwards to Bridgehouses, the planned double-bore tunnel at Woodhead was reduced to a single one and the Stalybridge branch dropped. The first sod was cut by Lord Wharncliffe on 1 October 1838, high on the Pennines at Salter's Brook. Several years were to elapse before the line's completion, but this period provided the town with an abundance of proposals for further railways, most of which failed, but one or two of which most certainly did not.

During 1843 efforts were made to revive interest in a direct line to Chesterfield. With the Manchester line now well and truly on the way the people of Sheffield needed very little pushing to demand better southbound connections. Accordingly, proposals were drawn up and presented to Parliament in March for a Sheffield & Chesterfield Junction Railway, but the select committee which was examining such proposals declared that its standing orders had not been complied with, and rejected the scheme on this technicality. One year later another public meeting was held, at the Cutlers' Hall, to push on with the attack yet again. But a most surprising turn of events occurred. From the floor of the meeting came an eloquently-argued proposal from Mr Henry Hinde, who persuaded all present that the interests of Sheffield would be far better served by building a new railway eastwards into Lincolnshire, instead of struggling to claw a way through the hills to the south. Discussions had already taken place during February 1844 regarding a possible eastwards extension from the SA&MR terminus via Masbrough to Gainsborough, but before anything was decided Hinde struck whilst the iron was hot. He pointed to the vast agricultural markets of Lincolnshire, the outlets for coal, limestone and steel and the cheap port of Gainsborough. The way south would also be opened up when London and York were connected by railway. The SA&MR was glad to hear

of his proposals as it favoured expansion of its own system beyond Bridgehouses. The Sheffield & Lincolnshire Junction Railway was floated publically on 7 March 1844, and several influential Sheffield men sat on the provisional committee. Lincoln was to be reached via Worksop and Retford, and the required capital was estimated at £650,000.

Railway politics of the time moved quickly, with many schemes meeting sudden death along the road to Parliament. But certain events forged alliances which were to last for long enough to benefit greatly all concerned. The next four years were to demonstrate these points well, starting in early 1844 when a powerful takeover bid of the SA&MR was initiated. This company was on very good terms in Manchester with its neighbour, the Manchester & Birmingham Railway. The two companies jointly promoted the Manchester, South Junction & Altrincham Railway, after which the M&B decided to attempt a leasing agreement over the SA&MR. Lacking sufficient capital, they approached Hudson's new Midland Railway for support. This was given readily and the three companies met at Normanton in October to discuss terms. The SA&MR was to be allowed to use Midland lines to the south, whilst the Midland gained a route to Manchester which was much shorter than the long-winded journey via Normanton and the Manchester & Leeds. After initially approving the scheme, the SA&MR shareholders caught cold feet when they realised that a joint effort between the M&B and its other ally, the London & Birmingham Railway, could divert virtually all northbound traffic away from their own town of Sheffield. Accordingly, they rejected the scheme entirely at a meeting held on 31 October. Had the move been successful then the SA&MR would have become yet another arm of Hudson's empire.

These events led to Hudson giving his support to the Sheffield & Lincolnshire Junction Railway proposals, as the new railway was actively supported by the SA&MR and could thus extend Hudson's tentacles well to the east if the leasing plan went ahead. After the takeover attempt failed, the SA&MR and the SLJR were left as close allies to fight off any alternative eastbound railway schemes. The first challenge came soon enough in the form of the Gainsborough, Sheffield & Chesterfield Railway, a proposal with support from the Manchester & Leeds Railway. A line to Gainsborough was planned from Wakefield via Tickhill, with an extension off to Chesterfield thrown in as a carrot to Sheffield supporters. This idea was seized upon by those who had seen the Sheffield & Chesterfield Junction Railway thrown out in the previous year. The GSCR promoters were quite happy to bypass Retford and Worksop in order to save seven miles on the run to Lincoln, and intended building a station in Sheffield (near the canal basin) at a sufficiently high level to get a good start on the climb out to Chesterfield.

Public meetings to discuss the choice of routes to Lincolnshire and the new Chesterfield line were held at Rotherham in October 1844 and in Sheffield during the following month. The second 'Railway Mania' was beginning, and the people of Rotherham clamoured for the GSCR to come via Masbrough and Westgate before heading east for Tickhill. (A far cry from their fears regarding the Sheffield & Rotherham Railway of less than 10 years before!) The Sheffield meeting generally approved of the GSCR plan for Lincoln, but Chesterfield was the jewel in the eye of the meeting. Routes were completely unsurveyed and still left largely to the imagination, but the support

drawn for both schemes caused a few wallets to flutter amongst the SA&MR and SLJR shareholders. Hinde and his colleagues were still winning support from all the towns and villages along the SLJR's route however, and the SA&MR was determined to back them to the hilt and so protect its menaced terminus. The Manchester & Leeds Railway was a deadly enemy of the Sheffield company, and so no protégé of the M&LR was to be allowed anywhere near the eastern counties.

A combination of the SA&MR's determination and Hinde's foresight and enthusiasm quickly steamrollered the GSCR's Lincolnshire scheme, and the latter company re-formed as the Manchester, Sheffield & Midland Junction Railway in order to put all its efforts into building a Chesterfield line. The eminent railway engineer William Cubitt was to supervise the construction,

Below: **The Gainsborough, Sheffield & Chesterfield Junction Railway and associated schemes.**

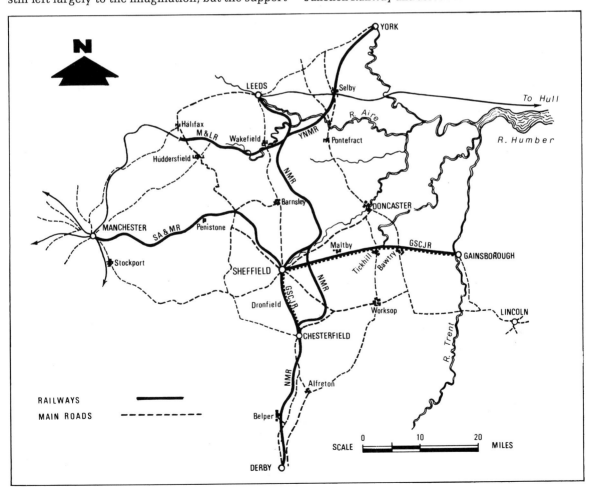

estimated to cost £750,000. This was undoubtedly a worthwhile scheme, and would have reduced the distance to Chesterfield from 22 miles via Masbrough (or 16 miles via a connection at Beighton to the MR from the proposed SLJR) to only 12 miles. The MSMJR intended to work from the SA&MR station via Dronfield. In the summer of 1845 the scheme went to Parliament, but, rather strangely, was lost on account of allegedly severe gradients. The maximum was two miles at 1 in 80, which even in 1845 no longer presented a fearsome obstacle to the locomotives then available. The Duke of Norfolk had objected to the plan, apparently worried over his coal and hay markets. The MSMJR promoters were baffled, and suspected some interference by Hudson.

Nevertheless, they were sure of ultimate success and decided to ease the gradients, liaise with the Duke and try again during the 1846 session. In January 1846 the Duke decided to back the SLJR scheme, including the MR connection southwards, as he felt this would best benefit the interests of Sheffield. Despite the loss of a powerful potential ally, the MSMJR went for its Act again, but once more lost due to the gradient question. Despite having a much shorter line, the curves and climbs were felt sure to rob any saving of journey times compared to the SLJR connection. The need for assistant locomotives for the climb out of Sheffield, and the apparent lack of arrangements for good connections and through running to the south, were further points laid against the MSMJR.

This gradient problem generated strong disbelief, and much local correspondence ensued. Public opinion pointed the finger of suspicion at the Duke, but the matter was never fully resolved. Cheap coal from Chesterfield would probably have been unwelcome amongst the Duke's Sheffield pits, and the line would have passed over seven miles of land owned by the Dukes of Rutland and Devonshire, who presumably would have been only too happy for an outlet to Sheffield. So nearly won but so sadly lost, the line was not revived until 20 years later, when an almost identical route was followed by the Midland Railway.

Looking eastwards again, the SLJR was quickly becoming one of the second Railway Mania's great success stories. One last attempt for an alternative scheme (via Bawtry) was firmly crushed by a lively public meeting in August 1845, and the SLJR was put before Parliament. The Standing Orders Committee expressed its favour for the line, but shortage of time delayed passage of the Bill until 3 August 1846. Work started immediately, with £175,000 being spent at Beighton, expected to be the scene of the heaviest works.

By this time the SA&MR had become a reality in Sheffield. At the end of October 1844, 100,000cu yd of earthworks at Wortley and 30,000cu yd at Wharncliffe remained to be done, whilst ballasting was making good progress elsewhere. In Sheffield, Miller & Blackie was constructing the final 600yd to Bridgehouses, and the pilot drift through Pye Bank Tunnel was being widened out. The last two drifts up at Woodhead met during January 1845, although the workings were clearly not going to be completed in time to allow through running between Manchester and Sheffield. The directors announced the line would be open to Dunford from 14 July with the tunnel being completed during August. The accompanying timetable was given, using an omnibus connection between Dunford and Woodhead:

Sheffield-Manchester/Manchester-Sheffield

Sheffield	dep	07.25	09.25	12.25	16.25	17.25
Wadsley Bridge		07.33	09.33	12.33	16.33	17.33
Oughty Bridge		07.40	09.40	12.40	16.40	17.40
Deep Car		07.49	09.49	12.49	16.49	17.49
Wortly		07.54	09.54	12.54	16.54	17.54
Penistone		08.06	10.06	13.06	17.06	18.06
Dunford	arr	08.18	10.18	13.18	17.18	18.18
Woodhead	dep	09.25	11.25	14.25	18.25	19.25
Hadfield		09.38	11.38	14.38	18.38	19.38
Dinting		09.45	11.45	14.45	18.45	19.45
Mottram		09.51	11.51		18.51	19.51
Newton		10.00	12.00	14.55	19.00	20.00
Dukinfield		10.06	12.06	15.01	19.06	20.06
Guide Bridge		10.10	12.10	15.05	19.10	20.10
Fairfield		10.16	12.16	—	19.16	20.16
Gorton		—	12.19	—	—	20.19
Ardwick		10.23	12.23	15.13	19.23	20.23
Manchester	arr	10.26	12.26	15.16	19.26	20.26
Manchester	dep		09.45	13.00	16.00	18.00
Ardwick			09.48	13.03	16.03	18.03
Gorton			09.52	—	—	—
Fairfield			09.57	13.10	—	—
Guide Bridge			10.04	13.17	16.15	18.15
Dukinfield			10.07	13.20	—	—
Newton			10.13	13.26	16.22	18.22
Mottram			10.22	13.35	16.31	18.31
Dinting			10.28	13.41	16.40	18.37
Hadfield			10.33	13.46	16.42	18.42
Woodhead	arr		10.53	14.06	17.00	19.00
Dunford	dep	08.45	12.00	15.13	18.07	20.07
Penistone		08.57	12.12	15.25	18.19	20.19
Wortley		09.07	12.22	15.35	18.29	20.29
Deep Car		09.12	12.27	15.40	18.34	20.34
Oughty Bridge		09.20	12.35	15.48	18.42	20.42
Wadsley Bridge		09.26	12.41	15.54	18.48	20.48
Sheffield	arr	09.31	12.46	15.59	18.53	20.53

On 9 July the Sheffield directors had a tour along the line, departing from Bridgehouses at 09.25 in a single wagon hauled by an unknown locomotive. The little train was suitably decorated and cheered by large crowds at Sheffield and Penistone. After meeting the Manchester directors they inspected the tunnel (where 280yd remained to be dug out) and then dined at the *Stanhope Arms* in Dunford. The Government Inspector of Railways, Maj-Gen Pasley, pronounced the line as being satisfactory on the 12 July, after a rather haphazard trip in an eight-coach train which departed 1hr 30min late and left several officials behind at Bridgehouses. The public opening took place without much ceremony; indeed the first

departure at 07.25 was more of a works train. The stations along the line had only recently been established with permanent staff, and this train delivered to all locations such impedimenta as ticket boxes, stamping machines, flags, ladders, and uniforms for porters and policemen. The return journey was faced with a serious obstacle between Wortley and Deep Car, where a section of track had yet to be laid! After the 09.25 departure had passed, the train reversed on to the down line and proceeded to the next crossover.

During these early days of operation some tender-first running was done, and this caused some apprehension to a Mr Wiley during a journey he made to Dunford in August. This form

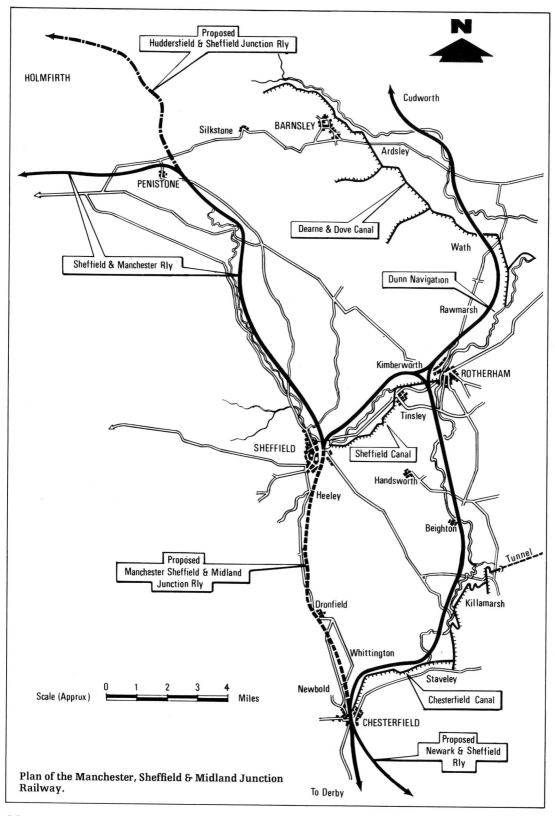

Plan of the Manchester, Sheffield & Midland Junction Railway.

HOLMFIRTH

Above: **The MSLR eastbound exit from Sheffield. Class 47 No 47.052 heads away from the city at Woodburn Junction with an Edinburgh and Glasgow-Nottingham express in September 1982.** *S. R. Batty*

Right: **The scenery at Darnall today bears no resemblance to the rural surroundings which existed in 1846. Class 47 No 47.506 speeds through the station with a Glasgow-Nottingham express in September 1982.** *S. R. Batty*

of running had been blamed for the deaths of two men on the S&R in 1841, and Mr Wiley became uneasy when he discovered that his fellow traveller was none other than the Sheffield coroner, Mr Badger! Apparently he did not share Mr Badger's confidence in the SA&MR, of which the latter was also a director.

Day return tickets were available, and these must have provided most of the SA&MR's income for the rest of the year. Very little goods traffic was carried until the Woodhead tunnel was finally opened from 23 December 1845. This event took place in very wintry surroundings which deterred many of the 200 invited guests from joining the first through departure for Manchester. The return arrival at 15.30 was greeted by bands playing and bells ringing, to celebrate the completion of a dream over 30 years old.

Promotion of the SLJR scheme was running at a very high pitch by 1846, and after the Act was passed in August no time was lost in getting the line built. Ultimately this would offer alternative routes to London, either via Lincoln and Peterborough or by meeting the Midland at Beighton. The Midland service to London via Masbrough

had deteriorated to an appalling level, with connections being either non-existent or extremely long-winded. Mail train timings were liable to summary alteration, much to the disgust of the business community which found its effective working day being altered constantly. The S&R-inspired Spital Hill connection from Wicker to Bridgehouses was started by the Midland, and the SA&MR decided that its station would be unable to cope with this extra traffic plus that from the future SLJR line. A decision was soon taken to build a new station a little farther eastwards, and this would be constructed along with the SLJR workings immediately outside Bridgehouses. This was to be a massive piece of civil engineering, and nearly five years were to elapse before Victoria station was completed.

Miller & Blackie was contracted to build the first section out to Beighton in October 1846, but this did not include the heavy works already mentioned near Bridgehouses. On a wet 15 October the first sod was cut at Darnall by Samuel Butcher, Sheffield's Mayor. The final link was now being commenced in a line of continuous railway across the country, and the section eastwards from Manchester to Grimsby became united under the new, single control of the Manchester, Sheffield & Lincolnshire Railway from 1 January 1847. The MSLR was formed by amalgamation of the SA&MR, the SLJR and the Great Grimsby & Sheffield Junction Railway, quickly agreed by all participants after the SA&MR's escape from amalgamation with the Hudson empire. (The GGSJR ran from Grimsby via Brigg to Gainsborough, where connection with the SLJR was made.) The Grimsby Dock Co intended co-operating fully with the GGSJR, and amidst the welter of schemes being dreamt up during the Mania of 1845 such an amalgamation made any interference by outside interests very unlikely. The SA&MR shareholders agreed to the proposal in December 1845, but pressure of work did not allow the new MSLR to hold its first meeting until 6 January 1847.

By early 1848 work was in hand on the line to Beighton, but the nature of the Wicker arches and the great viaduct required across the Rother Valley beyond Woodhouse soon forced the MSLR to revise its estimated date of completion from April of that year to January 1849. These civil engineering features caused long delays, and left a trail of death and broken bodies along the line. In February 1848 a mobile hoist (or 'traveller') being used to lift stone blocks up to rail level at the Wicker arches collapsed and dragged down 39ft of scaffolding. Two men were killed instantly and two died later. In May, an 18-year old youth was run over by some spoil wagons at Handsworth, near the tunnel then being built, and a man fell from the Wicker arches and drowned in the Don during August. Work along the rest of the line was going well though, and the MSLR felt confident enough to announce its expected opening of the new line in September — the next month!

But fate then took a hand, delivering two blows which were to delay the completion until the following summer. Heavy rainfall during September caused more than normal settlement of one of the arches which had been completed across the valley at Beighton. Despite flooding to a depth of 5ft, work was started on securing the piers. On 30 September the arch collapsed, killing three men and injuring another. Many more casualties would have occurred if the bad weather had not caused many men to be laid off. Like a row of

dominoes all the remaining 20 completed arches of the planned 36 collapsed, leaving the 440yd structure as a heap of rubble 40ft down in the valley. The connecting spur down to the MR had been laid, but the viaduct repairs were estimated to cost £17,000. The second blow came in October, when the third arch from the eastern end of the 700yd Wicker viaduct collapsed, fortunately without loss of life or injury. The wet weather was once again blamed, as heavy rainfall had washed out much of the arch's grouting.

A hectic pace followed during the rest of the year, and the last stone was keyed into the Wicker viaduct on 12 December, so completing the largest piece of masonry then built in the UK. The opening ceremony was attended by Bartolomé and Blake, two of the Sheffield directors, and the first locomotive crossed the viaduct on 16 December. Col Wynne inspected the new line from Bridgehouses through to its junction with the Midland via the Woodhouse-Beighton spur on 9 February 1849, paying especial attention to the Wicker arches' crossing of the road, River Don and canal which lay below. The section from here to Effingham Lane had been built rather wider, to accommodate the Victoria station, still in course of erection. Climbing at 1 in 155 through Darnall station to a summit just before the 374yd tunnel at Handsworth, the line then fell at 1 in 130-150 to the Midland main line at Beighton. This connection was expected to save 30min on the journey to Chesterfield compared with the route via Masbrough. Wynne was accompanied by seven MSLR directors (including Henry Hinde), and the party travelled in two coaches hauled by the locomotive *Vesta*. From Woodhouse Junction could be seen the ruin of the Rother viaduct and the feverish activity involved in driving adequate piles into the valley floor.

Public services commenced on 12 February, with seven trains running to Eckington and six in the reverse direction daily. The easternmost parts of the MSLR had all been completed by this time,

Top right: **Class 20 locomotives Nos 20.055 and 20.034 take a string of empty wagons past the site of Beighton station, on the descent from Woodhouse to the former NMR main line.** *S. R. Batty*

Centre right: **A view of the Wicker arches in 1903. Victoria station is to the right of the arch.** *H. Clayton collection*

Right: **Oughtybridge station in 1893, looking towards Penistone.** *R. Milnes/GCRS*

and the rebuilding of the Rother viaduct to allow through running to Grimsby was completed in time to allow a party of directors to make the journey from Manchester on 16 July 1849. The six-coach train was hauled by 2-2-2 *Jenny Lind* and arrived at Bridgehouses just before noon, where six directors joined their colleagues from Manchester and Liverpool. *Jenny Lind* then hauled the train on a 2hr run to Grimsby, and despite developing a tube leak she was coaxed up to 60mph along the way. A public timetable came into operation on the next day, with timetables and fares being advertised to Gainsborough, Grimsby and Hull (via the New Holland ferry) and also to London via two alternative routes — either by the Midland main line from Eckington, or via Gainsborough, Lincoln, Peterborough and Cambridge.

Hence the ambitions of the SA&MR, SLJR and GGSJR had all reached fruition under the common banner of the MSLR. Sheffield was now well and truly on the railway map (despite the lack of a direct Chesterfield line), and the opening of Victoria station on 15 September 1851 gave the two a truly worthy monument to its status in railway matters. The station, placed above a fairground and the Old Blonk Dam, was approached from Blonk Street via 320yd long, 50ft wide road inclined uphill at 1 in 30. Stairway access was provided from street level at Wicker. The 400ft frontage was rock-faced with Greenmore stone and Ashlar facings were quarried locally at Wadsley. One platform structure 1,000ft×40ft was provided, with bays at each end. An iron and glass verandah roof covered an area 400ft×83ft and collected rainwater for use in the lavatories. Four tracks ran through the station, two via the platforms and two being used for standing rolling stock. The bay platforms were intended to provide quick transfers for passengers between MSLR trains and MR connections departing for Beighton and Eckington. Two goods lines also ran around the rear of the station, behind the north wall. Some work remained to be done, but the public opening was accompanied by the customary waving of flags, playing of bands and despatching of special trains. The latter left for Grimsby and Hull (500 passengers), Worksop (2,000 souls crammed in) and London (described merely as 'well-filled'!). The capacity of the station for handling several trains was well proven when, at one point, two through trains and two Eckington trains were present. The contractor who had built the station (and also the town's new Market Hall) was a Mr Carlisle. He had also been responsible for the building (and subsequent rebuilding) of the Rother viaduct, and celebrated the occasion with great relief by providing his 500 navvies with beef, ham and beer. The original, rather gloomy terminal at Bridgehouses was expected to be fitted out as a goods depot within three months.

By this time railway political matters were polarising various companies into alliances and attitudes which soon became apparent in the services offered. In 1846 the infant Great Northern Railway had secured running powers over the SLJR from Retford to Sheffield, partly due to its agreement to build the last few miles of the SLJR to Lincoln (for joint use with the MSLR) and partly as a consolation prize from Parliament for failing to have its own Sheffield line approved. Across the

Below: **Victoria station and hotel in the early 1850s.** *Sheffield City Library*

Below right: **The ex-SYR line, looking from Blackburn Valley Junction towards Meadow Hall & Wincobank. Buffer stops are now fitted just to the left of the picture.** *S. R. Batty*

country the LNWR was planning to capture all traffic to the Midlands and North, and saw the GNR as its principal foe. Seeking allies for the struggle ahead, the LNWR General Manager, Capt Mark Huish, quickly came to understandings with the Midland and Lancashire & Yorkshire Railways. The MSLR worked closely with the LNWR in Manchester and with the Midland Railway around Sheffield, but would have nothing to do with the LYR. Consequently the company became involved in the infamous Euston Square Confederacy, formalised in December 1849 and effective from 1 February 1850 with the sole intention of killing off the GNR. Part of the agreement gave the MSLR a monopoly of the Hull traffic, but the price to be paid was that it would not send GNR traffic to the port, and would charge full rates if the GNR ever used its running powers to reach Sheffield. Many people involved with the MSLR resented this state of affairs, seeing the GNR as a potential profitable ally which would expand alongside the 'Sheffield'. The LNWR was a far-off concern which had a reputation for autocracy and poor service, whilst the LYR was, quite simply, beyond the pale.

In 1850 the GNR took up its running powers by announcing through trains from Lincoln (using the joint MSLR metals) to the capital from 7 August, via its own main line to King's Cross. From January 1851 it started taking goods traffic from Bridgehouses, appointing Mrs Sarah Lister of 104 Eyre Street as agent. July saw the Midland introduce through services from Bridgehouses to Euston Square via Eckington, departures leaving at 11.00, 13.40 and 20.55 and return trains leaving London at 06.30, 09.15 and 10.15. The Great Exhibition of that year encouraged the GNR to grasp the nettle and announce excursion trains to London. The Midland ran its own excursion train daily from Bridgehouses at 11.30 with cheap

return fares of 15s (75p), 10s (50p), and 5s (25p), for first, second and third class travel respectively. Promptly, the GNR matched these prices, and Bridgehouses choked with customers. But then the MSLR invoked the Confederacy agreement and demanded 5s 8d ($28\frac{1}{2}$p) from the GNR for every 5s fare it carried! Having previously paid 2s 11d ($14\frac{1}{2}$p) to the MSLR, the GNR cut its losses and withdrew from any Sheffield traffic. The MSLR shame-facedly excused itself by saying that a proportional toll would not cover any of the costs involved in accommodating the GNR traffic. No benefits of this move were seen by the MSLR shareholders, and the unhappy rejection of the GNR and unwanted alliance with the LNWR stumbled along. Evidence of double-dealing came to light in 1853 when the LNWR was seen to be trying to reduce the MSLR to little more than a branch line in status. The Confederacy finally tumbled in May 1857 upon the threat of legal action by a Leeds director of the GNR, and the MSLR quickly severed all ties with the LNWR and gladly buried the hatchet with the GNR.

Through trains from King's Cross to Sheffield and Manchester via Retford began running from 1 August, with two trains daily each way taking only 5hr 20min to connect the two cities. These 'Manchester Flyers' left King's Cross at 10.00 and 17.30, with the up trains leaving London Road at 09.55 and 17.20. The 'Flyers' called at Victoria at 13.50, 21.21, 11.15 and 18.43 respectively, further up trains departing at 06.20 (arr King's Cross 12.45), 11.05 (16.00) and 13.17 (18.00), and down trains leaving London at 08.45 (arr Victoria 12.50), 11.00 (15.50) and 13.40 (20.15). An up mail train left at 23.00 to arrive at 03.30, whilst the day mails travelled down on the 08.45 from King's Cross. Hope was expressed that the day mail could go up by the 11.15 'Flyer' instead of the 11.00 train, so giving an extra 45min

Above: **English Electric Type 4 No D208 breasts the summit on to the main line at Woodburn Junction with a Hull-Sheffield (Victoria) train on 11 October 1958.** *K. R. Pirt*

delivery time in London! So began a long period of MSLR/GNR co-operation, which gave Sheffield a good London service which was not to be excelled until the opening of the GCR London extension over 40 years later.

Meanwhile the town gained another passenger service by virtue of a small railway which had opened its line to the north of Sheffield. This was the South Yorkshire Railway, running westwards from Doncaster to Swinton and then using running powers over the Midland main line down to Wicker. The SYR was originally promoted in 1845 with the strong support of the SA&MR, which had an eye on the locomotive coal traffic to be taken from the area. John Parker was appointed as a provisional director to safeguard SA&MR interests, but some years were to pass before matters were to its entire satisfaction. The plans were thrown out of Parliament during 1846, but were then resubmitted with branches off the Doncaster-Barnsley line to Elsecar, Rotherham and Penistone. The scheme was then accepted, but with only the first branch line being allowed. During August 1847 the SYR held its first meeting, at the Tontine Hotel in Sheffield, and in November it transferred offices from Doncaster to Norfolk Street. Opening of the first section from Doncaster to Swinton took place on 10 November 1849, with the service down to Wicker being operated by the Midland due to the SYR's complete lack of passenger stock. Trains left Wicker at 08.00, 11.10, 14.15 and 17.45. In the summer of 1851 the SYR commenced work on building the Blackburn Valley line, leaving its Mexborough-Barnsley section at Aldam Junction and heading south on a single line (doubled by 1876) to meet the Midland at Blackburn Valley Junction, between Brightside and Wincobank on the former S&R. Reversal at Aldam Junction would allow a through Sheffield-Chapeltown-Barnsley service, but difficulties with the MR over the increasing use of Wicker station delayed the introduction of this service until 9 September 1854, nine months after the line's completion. Three trains daily were provided each way:

Sheffield-Barnsley/Barnsley-Sheffield

Sheffield	dep	08.23	15.00	18.40
Brightside		08.25	15.05	18.46
Chapeltown & Thorncliffe		08.48	15.28	19.08
Westwood & Mortomley		09.01	15.41	19.21
Smithly & Darley Main		09.09	15.49	19.29
Ardsley		09.22	16.02	19.42
Barnsley	arr	09.30	16.10	19.50

Barnsley	dep	07.00	09.40	17.20
Ardsley		07.07	09.47	17.27
Smithly & Darley Main		07.21	10.01	17.41
Westwood & Mortomley		07.30	10.10	17.50
Chapeltown & Thorncliffe		07.42	10.22	18.02
Brightside		08.05	10.45	18.25
Sheffield	arr	08.10	10.50	18.30

The station at Meadow Hall & Wincobank, between Brightside and Chapeltown & Thorncliffe, was not opened until May 1868, and in 1875 a 1¾-mile branch to Grange colliery was opened from Grange Lane station.

The lifeblood of the SYR was, of course, coal. With this traffic in mind the GNR had taken a quarter share in the SYR, and during the early 1850s had started leasing proposals for a complete takeover. The Midland Railway objected vigorously, and demanded a share of all such traffic. This proved to be the last straw for the GNR, which was having some difficulty in living with the rather eccentric ways of the SYR, and in 1853 it abandoned any ideas of amalgamation completely. Enter now the MSLR, which by 1855 had opened its Birley colliery branch from Woodhouse Junction and was finding its feet in the coal haulage business. By 1860 the SYR had plans for its own line from Meadow Hall Junction on the Barnsley line to a new terminus near Sheffield's canal basin, close to Victoria. The MSLR stepped in and offered the use of Victoria (saving the SYR £40,000 building costs), to be reached by bringing the SYR line due south to a junction with the MSLR at Woodburn. Seeing the chance of sending coal and minerals from the SYR as far afield as Grimsby and Birkenhead, the MSLR offered lease negotiations much as the GNR had done, and these were approved by the shareholders in February 1861 by 6,103 votes in favour to 1,264 against. The GNR, which had sulked since 1853, felt rather put out by not being involved in the deal, but the MSLR assured it of fair and equal treatment regarding the future traffic. Work on the Sheffield extension went ahead from early 1861, but various difficulties

with land purchases delayed progress considerably. Legal wrangles over the proposed Woodburn junction halted work completely for a time, but matters were resolved by a suitable Act of Parliament dated July 1862. To be fair, the SYR had only itself to blame for most of these delays, as much of the work went ahead without giving any consideration to owner's rights or any necessary Acts which may have been needed. Indeed, the latter were regarded as hindrances best avoided! Full transfer of the SYR to the MSLR took place on the day of the final opening, 1 August 1864. One intermediate station only was provided, at Broughton Lane, but Tinsley followed in March 1869 and Attercliffe in August 1871. All passenger services between Sheffield, Barnsley and Doncaster were thus transferred from Wicker to Victoria.

A ¼-mile goods branch had been laid in from just east of Victoria to a point almost due south of the station in 1855, but the depot (called Park Goods) was not provided until 1865. The Spital Hill Tunnel connection to Wicker from Bridgehouses was the scene of a tragedy on 25 February 1861. The land above the tunnel had been leased to Messrs Hunt & Co, who started to build stables and warehouses on the property. The MR had insisted that no building should take place within 20ft of the arch centre, and the nearest wall was outside this limit when work started. During the excavations it became necessary to replace the soil between this

Below: **Ex-WD 'Austerity' 2-8-0 No 90582 passes Broughton Lane with an up coal train on 12 May 1956.** *T. G. Hepburn/Rail Archive Stephenson*

partially-built wall and the exposed south side of the tunnel roof with rubble. Whilst this was being done several men who were standing on the wall felt it start to collapse, and jumped clear, away from the tunnel. Six men leapt on to the tunnel roof, which then fell in and was quickly followed by the north side of the tunnel roof. All six men — James Malloy, John Harriman, Samuel Lawton, and Thomas, William and Henry Booth — were killed.

The last piece of main line construction by the MSLR in the area was a northward extension from the SYR line at Tinsley towards Rotherham. This would give direct access to Doncaster and a much deeper penetration of the coalfield. Work started in late 1864 and the estimated cost of the line was only £80,000, because much of the land to be used was already owned by the MSLR by virtue of the SYR having taken over the River Dun Navigation Co in 1850. The route was to follow the canal closely and thus avoid unnecessary land purchase. However, certain parcels of land did have to be bought, and a great deal of work became necessary to divert the river and provide new locks along the canal. The original estimate was rapidly swallowed up and probable expenditure raced towards the £250,000 level. When the full realisation of this horror dawned, the MSLR promptly stopped all work and paused for thought. Amidst this financial disaster, an offer of assistance was suddenly made in late 1867 from a most

unexpected source — the London & North Western Railway.

Despite already having running powers over the MSL from Ardwick Junction, Manchester, to Sheffield (Victoria), the LNWR was planning a new line from Chapel-en-le-Firth to Sheffield via the Hope Valley. This scheme actually received Parliament's approval, but to fight off this new main line the MSLR urged the LNWR to use to the full its existing running powers via Woodhead, which until this time had been rarely invoked. Seeing the chance to reach Sheffield easily and without involving construction of either a main line or a station, the LNWR agreed, and dropped the Hope Valley plans. The MSLR then offered to share the costs of building the Rotherham line, including any improvements needed at Victoria, with the ultimate aim of joint ownership and a tentacle with which to reach the coalfield. Parliament, however, had other ideas. The Bill went forward in 1868 and was rejected, the LNWR gaining neither joint ownership nor running powers beyond Victoria. Construction did go ahead though, and the line opened to a temporary terminus in Rotherham in August 1868. Fifteen weekday trains ran daily in each direction, passing under the Midland at Masbrough South Junction and under the former S&R line near the latter's Westgate terminus. The temporary Rotherham station was rebuilt soon afterwards, and was known as Rotherham (Central) from February 1874.

Left: **Tinsley station and Tinsley South Junction c1947.**
D. Thompson

Right: **An up train of empty hopper wagons near Broughton Lane behind a Class 37 Co-Co locomotive.**
S. R. Batty

Centre right: **Tinsley South Junction in 1983, with Class 08 No 08.878 returning from a foray along the remains of the SYR Barnsley line. This branch now goes only as far as the coking plant at Smithywood.**
S. R. Batty

Bottom: **At Rotherham Main, the MSLR Rotherham line passed below the Midland main line south of Masbrough South Junction. Class 31 No 31.301 heads south along the 'Old Road' with a train of empty iron ore tipplers on 31 October 1977.**
C. R. Davies

2 1870-1922 — Growth and Development

After the failure of the Manchester, Sheffield & Midland Junction Railway scheme in July 1846, no further action was taken regarding a direct line from the town to Chesterfield. However, in the early 1860s the long fed-up railway users of the town once again picked up the cudgels and prepared themselves for another battle to win this long-needed arterial connection. The station at Wicker was hopelessly inadequate both in serving the existing traffic and in offering any possibility of improvement. The buildings were jammed in on all sides by works and factories, and the track layout could not be stretched to give any relief. (The Midland must have been glad to see the SYR defect to Victoria and so allow a little breathing space.) Passengers for the MR main line still had to face long waits and uncertain connections at Masbrough, just as they had done so in 1840. True to the style of the day, a public meeting was held on 5 December 1862 to discuss further the 'railway communications of the town.' The MR was informed of the intended meeting but did not attend. Its Chairman, Samuel Beale, wrote to the Mayor to assure the meeting that the directors had resolved, 'if assured of the support of the town' to 'recommend their shareholders to apply, in the session of 1864, for an Act for a direct line from the Midland Railway near Chesterfield, to Dronfield and Sheffield.' The route would be four miles shorter than going via Masbrough, and much faster. 1864 was the earliest date by which the scheme could be submitted, as the present session of Parliament was too far advanced, and the MR had its hands full (mainly with the building of St Pancras station) during 1863.

Some degree of mutual mistrust was present however; the MR went to some length to explain that it was acting in good faith, perhaps feeling unsure of complete support for its line. The public meeting agreed to form an independent company to work with the MR to ensure the town *did* get its railway, and on terms which would be acceptable to all concerned. The company would not only apply pressure to the Midland when this was felt

to be needed, but would be able to go ahead with the line independently should the MR falter in any way. At a meeting held in Derby during February 1863 the MR told the committee that £500,000 had been allocated to the scheme, but would not show any plans or proposals to the Sheffield men, fearing that any opponents might benefit from such knowledge and also that land prices along the route would escalate. The committee hinted vaguely at proposals for an alternative route to the city from Derbyshire, but would not enlarge upon this when requested by the rather ruffled Midland. Whether this was a reference to the proposed LNWR Hope Valley scheme, or to another genuine rival scheme, or whether it was just a ploy to keep the Midland on its toes is not known, but before very long the MR's worst suspicions were confirmed.

In June 1863 the Midland issued some hurriedly-prepared plans which, although lacking in detail, showed the line entering the environs on leaving Bradway Tunnel (1 mile 264yd), 'emerging into the valley of the Sheaf at Twenty-Well Sink Lane, a little to the west of Beauchieff Hall. . . .' On 10 July the plan for the new station was seen, and the committee thought it 'too far from the business part of the town' and 'the approaches to it very defective.' Crossley, of the Midland, agreed to make various changes as requested. These resulted in plans being made for a large station above the River Sheaf from Pond Forge Bridge to a point opposite Harmer Lane. Civil engineering works would involve 1.2million cub yd of embankments, a similar amount of cuttings, a 260yd viaduct and 2,000yd of tunnel. Costs were estimated at £40/yd for tunnelling, £60/yd for viaducts and 1s/cu yd of earthworks.

With matters apparently settled to the satisfaction of all concerned, the Midland must have been thunderstruck by the events of the next month. On 20 August a meeting was held in Sheffield Town Hall at which a competitive line from Sheffield to the south and west was promoted. Known as the Sheffield, Chesterfield, Bakewell, Ashbourne, Staf-

Above: **A Class 31 hauls a train of ballast empties past Treeton South in early 1982. MAS resignalling work was in progress at the time.** *S. R. Batty*

ford & Uttoxeter Junction Railway, its objectives were to reach the LNWR at Stafford, provide only a branch to Chesterfield and improve communications to the West Midlands and beyond. A station would be built in Townhead Street, and the meeting supported the scheme readily. Its staunchest protagonists were the Mayor (John Brown of Atlas Steelworks fame), the Town Council and the Cutlers' Co, but many industrialists present did not vote. The line was seen as a good buy at a cost of £1 million, a figure put forward by Brassey & Field, one of the great railway contractors of the day. This firm offered to put up £700,000 of capital if the meeting would subscribe the remainder, but what strings would be attached was not made clear. The 46-mile single line would leave Sheffield almost along the MR proposed route, but from Beauchieff would swing towards Totley and Baslow. Many tunnels,

cuttings and viaducts would have been needed and would have mopped up a large portion of the estimated cost. Running powers would be granted to the Midland, in return for the use of the latter company's entire system. Needless to say, the Midland rejected this proposal very firmly!

With the benefit of more than a century of hindsight, it would appear that delays with the Midland line and long memories of poor service provoked interest in the new line. Add to this a measure of speculation by Brassey & Field and also happy memories of the lucrative SLJR scheme (which gave similar access to new markets across the country for coal, iron, steel and minerals), and a very rosy picture of yet another burst of 'Mania' was painted. Several prominent Sheffield industrialists were behind the scheme, including John Brown, whose steelworks would certainly benefit from the proposal. A large number of people were quite happy to see the MR come via Dronfield, and the Staffordshire line seems to have been the idea of just a small number of very influential people. Both schemes went to Parliament in 1864, but after a lengthy

hearing the Staffordshire Bill floundered because of some rather unconventional financing. The company's capital was quoted as £1.5million, of which only £120,000 had been raised. Some careful questioning revealed that the remainder was in the form of a deposit granted by the Guardian Insurance Co, against an undertaking that the Guardian directors could control the Bill or even stop it at any time if they desired. This was felt to be undesirable, as Parliament insisted that both the capital and the Bill should be controlled by the company, and not by any outside agency.

Construction of the Midland line started very soon after Parliamentary approval, and over 1,000 recently-built houses on the approach to Sheffield were compulsorily purchased and then demolished. On the northbound exit from the town a planned tunnel had to be replaced by a cutting and 15 bridges when redundant coal and stone workings were discovered. The new station site involved considerable drainage and civil engineering work above the Rivers Porter and Sheaf. By August 1867 work on Bradway Tunnel was progressing from eight shafts, but no completion date could be given. Stations were built at Unston, Dronfield, Abbey Houses, Ecclesall and Heeley. Electricity was provided at most locations, including the new Pond Street station.

Capt Tyler inspected the line during January

Left: Beauchief & Abbeydale station in the 1890s. *Sheffield City Library*

Below left: Millhouses & Ecclesall in BR steam days. 'Royal Scot' No 46157 *The Royal Artilleryman* climbs past with a Newcastle-Bristol express on 4 July 1961. *J. M. Smith*

Right: The cavernous southbound exit from Midland station. *S. R. Batty*

Below: Class 45 No 45.012 threads its way through the cuttings north of Midland station on 30 June 1975. *L. A. Nixon*

Below right: Class 45 No 45.118 makes a smoky departure past Nunnery Junction with the 10.05 Weymouth-Leeds on 11 September 1982. *S. R. Batty*

1870, amidst appalling weather conditions, and the new route was opened publicly on 1 February. No ceremony of any sort was performed, and the first down train to arrive was the 06.15 from St Pancras which entered the town '... just as if it had been accustomed to do so at any time for the last 10 years.' The *Railway News* observed that '... spruce collectors asked you for your tickets, and slammed the door, and went their way, and left you to go yours.' The lack of the ceremony so loved by the Victorians on these occasions prompted the local press to remark '... we have witnessed more fuss over the opening of a drinking-fountain....' Contemporary descriptions tell of 'rock-faced wall stone, tool-dressed and in the style of architecture Grecian, with Gothic headings.' An iron and glass roof above the four 700ft × 30ft platforms was supported on 42 columns, and a 105ft footbridge was provided. Two open docks were built at the north end and one covered dock at the southern end. Three signalboxes were built, one actually on the platforms. Two express trains and four 'fasts' were sent to London daily, with 79 trains passing through the station each day. Goods and mineral traffic was routed via the original NMR route between Chesterfield (Tapton Junction) and Masbrough.

Four entrances to the station were provided off Howard Street, giving access to a booking hall and first and second class ladies' and gentlemen's waiting rooms. Two refreshment rooms were supervised by a Miss Halton 'plus six ladies and a host of waiters.' The Stationmaster was Mr Curtis, who transferred from Wicker and brought several staff with him. All the masonry and woodwork were provided by Chadwick & Thirlwell of Masbrough, and the ironwork by Close, Eyre & Co of York. As with so many public openings of the past, much work remained to be done. The approach from Old Haymarket was in a 'rough and dangerous' state, and the roads leading to the station were surrounded by 'dirty, dilapidated works and narrow streets.'

Leaving the station northwards the line travelled just over one mile to join the former S&R line at Grimesthorpe Junction. The only station on this short stretch was Attercliffe Road, perched high above street level on an embankment. This elevation prompted one traveller to observe that the station 'would give quite a good view of the town, but for the dense smoke, clouds of steam and belching furnaces.'

Pond Street goods depot was opened just south of the station on the down side of the line. To the

Above: **One of the shortened 'Trans-Pennine' units approaches Attercliffe station with the 11.23 Hull-Manchester (Piccadilly) on 1 October 1982.** *S. R. Batty*

Above right: **The 07.55 from Plymouth accelerates hard through Attercliffe on the last leg of its journey to Leeds on 1 October 1982.** *S. R. Batty*

Right: **Empty coaching stock from Midland station is propelled past Nunnery Single Line Junction into the ex-LMSR sidings by '4F' 0-6-0 No 43900 on 4 October 1958.** *K. R. Pirt*

Below: **The original MR/MSLR Nunnery connection, now disused, seen from Woodburn Junction.**
S. R. Batty

north, a Midland/MSLR connection was formed by an eastbound spur leaving the new line at Nunnery Main Line Junction and climbing at 1 in 45 to meet the MSLR, via a back-shunt, to the east of Victoria. As with the Spital Hill connection, this line does not seem to have been overburdened with traffic. A branch was put in to Nunnery colliery during 1886, but the connection with the MSLR became disused before the end of the century. However, this little line's usefulness was to be greatly exploited in much later years. At Rotherham a curve was laid in from Holmes Junction to give access for traffic from Sheffield to the NMR at Masbrough South Junction.

Further improvements during the 1870s took place mainly on the MSLR system. The original,

temporary station at Woodhouse was eventually replaced by a new structure 700yd farther west in October 1875. Two short connections were opened in 1873, the $\frac{1}{4}$-mile curve between Tinsley (East) and Tinsley (West) during July and the Attercliffe Junction-Darnall Junction curve in August. These lines allowed the South Yorkshire-Lincolnshire coal traffic to bypass Victoria and its immediate approaches and completed the Woodburn-Attercliffe-Darnall triangle, which was rarely used by passenger traffic until 1914. Despite starting improvements at Victoria and laying more sidings at Wadsley Bridge, the MSLR was accused by the manufacturers of the town of giving a poor service. Perhaps having bullied the Midland into building the new line, they felt the MSLR should be put under a little pressure! In response the MSLR spent more money at Victoria and set about increasing track capacity by improving selected bottlenecks. During the late summer of 1875 new passenger lines were opened at Woodburn, the ex-SYR single line was doubled between Meadow Hall and Chapeltown, and a third line put in between Broughton Lane and Tinsley. At nearby Rotherham events were largely confined to station alterations and renamings. On the S&R line a new station was opened at

Left: Class 37 No 37.093 passes Masbrough South with an up freight on 21 May 1976. *L. A. Nixon*

Below left: Class 46 No 46.015 approaches the site of Wincobank North Junction with the 10.12 Newcastle-Cardiff on 28 February 1977. *G. W. Morrison*

Above right: An MGR trainload of coal for Smithywood crosses on to the former SYR line at Meadow Hall Junction behind a Class 47 locomotive. *S. R. Batty*

Right: Tinsley West Junction in 1983, looking towards Tinsley South Junction and the location of the former Tinsley station. Passing under the M1 motorway viaduct is the single line connection to Tinsley East Junction. *S. R. Batty*

Left: Several generations of signwriting at Woodhouse. *S. R. Batty*

Left: Woodhouse station in 1910. *R. Milnes collection*

43

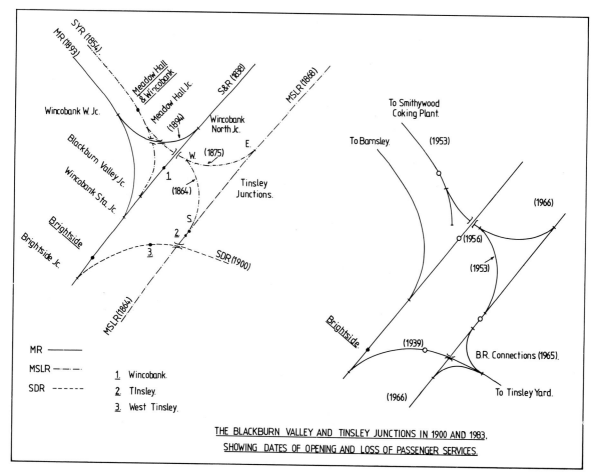

THE BLACKBURN VALLEY AND TINSLEY JUNCTIONS IN 1900 AND 1983.
SHOWING DATES OF OPENING AND LOSS OF PASSENGER SERVICES.

Wincobank on 1 April 1868, and the Rotherham terminus was replaced by a temporary structure c1872. This was finally named Rotherham (Westgate) in May 1896. Rotherham (Central), the MSLR's original 1874 station on the Tinsley-Mexborough extension, was renamed Rotherham & Masbrough from January 1889. Just to add the final touch of confusion to matters, the Midland's somewhat remote Masbrough station in the original S&R/NMR junction was renamed Masbrough & Rotherham from May 1896. This title lasted only 12 years, and in April 1908 the station received its perhaps most familiar name of Rotherham (Masbrough). Neepsend station on the former SA&MR was not opened until 1888, due to the MSLR being reluctant to pay the entire cost of bridging the Don to provide public access. After 40 years of agitation, the company and the corporation shared the bill of £1,900 and the small station was duly built. During 1883 the lease to the operators of the Victoria Hotel expired. It was not relet and the MSLR launched itself into a new field of management.

Above: **The Blackburn Valley and Tinsley Junctions.**
S. R. Batty

Right: **A Hull bound DMU passes Wincobank station Junction in icy conditions on 31 December 1978. The box closed during the following month.** *T. Dodgson*

The Midland's new Chesterfield line was involved in plans for an independent Dore & Chinley line in 1884, when the Dore & Chinley Railway received an Act to build a line westwards from Dore & Totley station (opened in 1872) to Chinley. Having got so far, the company found itself under-subscribed, and was glad to have the MR take over construction. The engineering work involved — notably tunnelling at Totley and Cowburn — delayed the opening of the line for goods traffic until November 1893 and for passenger traffic until the following June. In the town, Queen's Road goods depot was opened in June

1892, on a site a little to the south and on the same (down) side of the line as Pond Street goods depot. The Midland Railway's last development in the area concerned its own Blackburn Valley route to Barnsley, paralleling that of the MSLR as far as Chapeltown and never more than a quarter of a mile away to this point. Built initially to serve only the Thorncliffe ironworks, the line diverged from the main line between Brightside and Wincobank stations and opened for goods traffic on 30 August 1893. By this time, however, the MR had received Acts to extend the line to Barnsley West Junction from Chapeltown, a distance of $7\frac{3}{4}$ miles. Goods traffic was sent from 12 April 1897 and a full passenger service to Barnsley started from 1 July. Intermediate stations were provided at Ecclesfield, Chapeltown (both on the original 1893 branch), Wentworth & Hoyland Common, Elsecar & Hoyland and Wombwell. To give access to the branch from the Rotherham direction a new curve between Wincobank (West) and Wincobank (North) was laid in during 1896.

The 1890s saw the LNWR gain a foothold in handling the town's goods traffic. In May 1895 the company opened a $\frac{3}{4}$-mile branch eastwards from Woodburn Junction to Sheffield City goods terminal in Bernard Road alongside the largely unused MR/MSLR Nunnery connection. But the premier line was not for making do with an inadequate terminus buried amidst its rivals'

networks, and the LNWR soon obtained powers for a far more suitable establishment. A site was chosen at Broad Steet and Wharf Street, opposite the Corn Exchange, and the $\frac{3}{4}$-mile extension necessary from Bernard Road involved tunnelling beneath the Nunnery Colliery Railway and then bridging the Midland's northern exit. From here the line entered the depot on arches. The depot itself covered 94,260sq ft, on three floor levels, and used two 20-ton hydraulic lifts to lower wagons from rail level to basement warehouse level, a distance of nearly 30ft. Opening took place in February 1903, and Bernard Road depot was retained to deal with much heavier loads — 40ton could be handled there, compared to the new depot's maximum capability of only 10ton items. Nine sidings were built, and also a small engine shed which could accommodate six locomotives. To avoid confusion, the older depot was renamed Nunnery Goods and the new establishment took over the title of City Goods.

The MSLR commenced an important piece of new line with construction southwards from Beighton being sanctioned by an Act of 26 July 1889. This allowed building through to Annesley with a branch included to serve Chesterfield, so doing away with the need to run over MR metals from Beighton via Eckington in order to reach the town of the crooked spire. More importantly though, it was the start of the

Left: **A Manchester-Hull DMU approaches the site of Wincobank North Junction in March 1983. The disused viaduct to the left carried the goods-only connection to Wincobank West Junction until September 1969. Below this lies the truncated remains of the SYR line to Blackburn Valley Junction, now used as a wagon siding. In the immediate foreground, out of sight in a cutting, lies the ex-MR Barnsley line.** *S. R. Batty*

Centre left: **Dore & Totley station in the early 1900s, with a Midland 4-2-2 in the background heading for Chesterfield.** *Sheffield City Library*

Bottom left: **Five years after nationalisation, Compound No 41072 still carries LMSR lettering on her tender as she departs from Dore & Totley with a Derby local train on 9 May 1953.** *B. R. Goodlad*

Above right: **Class 4F No 44211 passes Dore & Totley Station Junction signalbox and enters the station with a Chinley stopper in September 1960.** *Ken Smith*

Right: **The remains of the former LNWR engine shed at Nunnery, closed during 1928 and seen here in late 1966.** *P. C. H. Robinson*

Below: **Wharf Street goods depot exterior in 1967.** *P. C. H. Robinson*

advance on London. The line was completed during 1892, with the new MSLR Sheffield-Beighton-Chesterfield service commencing on 4 June.

At about the same time another, smaller railway company was about to burst upon the scene. This was the Sheffield District Railway, a small company which never fulfilled its promise but which somehow survived a precarious existence to become a part of the present day network. Several Nottinghamshire landowners made plans for a line across the country from Warrington to Sutton-on-Sea, to give access to two ports for export of their coal. A branch northwards from Langwith would reach Beighton on the MSLR and tap the local collieries. None of the large companies wanted the new railway, and the MSLR rejected outright any suggestion of running powers into Victoria. The landowners seemingly had not a friend in the world, when suddenly the

Below: **The sad remains of the MSLR's 1892 line to Annesley. Closed to passenger traffic in 1966, the line is now singled and terminates at Arkwright colliery, near Chesterfield. Looking south from Beighton, the line crosses the Midland main line and curves out of sight towards Killamarsh.** *S. R. Batty*

Bottom: **An up fitted goods heads along the ex-GCR main line at Beighton behind 'B16/1' 4-6-0 No 61458.** *J. H. Turner*

Great Eastern Railway stepped forward and offered financial support in return for running powers. The GER could see a healthy coal and steel traffic being siphoned on to its own system via the proposed GNR/GER joint connection at Pyewipe Junction, Lincoln. So the new railway, known as the Lancashire, Derbyshire & East Coast Railway went to Parliament along with the MSLR's first 'London Extension' Bill. The LDECR was fully approved (and the 'Extension' Bill thrown out, much to the MSLR's fury) on 8 July 1891.

Capital, however, was not so readily forthcoming as approval, and here the GER played a trump card. Putting up £250,000, it placed a director on the board and insisted that work should go ahead

only on the Lincoln-Chesterfield and Langwith-Beighton sections. This would give the GER all the traffic it could carry off, and construction started in June 1892. Soon the remaining unstarted portions of the LDECR were formally abandoned, and developing relations with the MR saw the line from Langwith tied into the Midland at Beighton instead of to the MSLR at Killamarsh. This system eventually opened on 8 March 1897, without any separate connection through to Sheffield. Four businessmen then stepped in and formed a company to rectify matters. Sir George Reresby Sitwell, Mr Robert Fenwick Mills, Mr Peverill Turnbull and Alderman Gainsford found the LDECR short of cash, however, and the idea lapsed until 1896. Then the GER/LDECR decided

Above: **Beighton station and staff about 1893, looking north. The present PW yard is located on the right, beyond the platforms.** *R. Milnes/GCRS*

Right: **Uprated Class 47 No 47.601 accelerates an MGR train southwards at Treeton Junction on 28 March 1977. The present southeastern exit from Tinsley Yard has been built on the SDR's connection with the MR at this point.** *G. W. Morrison*

to build from the Killamarsh branch to a new goods depot at Attercliffe, hopefully to receive running powers from a short spur at Tinsley along the MSLR at Victoria. Unfortunately the MSLR's attitude had not mellowed over the years, and its solicitor, Worsley-Taylor, went so far as to say that the GER was using 'subversive' means to gain access to the town.

This was the initial form of the Sheffield District Railway, which received its Act as such on 4 August 1896. This line would have been little more than a dead-ended goods branch, but the Midland offered running powers along the 'Old Road' to Treeton and also from Brightside into Pond Street, leaving only the Treeton-Brightside section and a short line from there into Attercliffe goods depot to be built by the SDR. These proposals were accepted, and the first sod was cut at Attercliffe by the Duke of Norfolk on 20 November 1896. A short section was built from Killamarsh up to Beighton, as originally planned by the LDECR, and the entire line (built by C. J. Wills) was opened to the public on 21 May 1900. Two intermediate stations were provided, at Catcliffe and Tinsley Road. Crowds gathered all along the

line, and the entire proceedings were permeated with euphoria by an event reported from many miles away — the relief of the Boers' siege of Mafeking.

Physically the line was undemanding but crammed with civil engineering works. From Treeton the line climbed at 1 in 150 towards a summit near Tinsley. A nine-arch viaduct crossed the Rother just before Catcliffe station was reached (where future sidings were expected for the Waverley colliery), and the 80yd Brinsworth Tunnel was followed by deep cuttings until the Great Central Railway line from Rotherham was crossed on a steel girder bridge. Tinsley Road station (renamed Tinsley West from 1 July 1907) was soon to have sidings to Tinsley Park colliery which would take 250,000ton of coal each year, and from here a short gallop across the fields brought the trains to the massive Brightside viaduct. This crossed the Don and also Meadow Hall Road, and employed six spans of 30ft, a 100ft lattice girder and an 80ft plate girder section in doing so. Brightside Junction connected with Midland metals, and running powers down to Sheffield District Junction (later renamed Attercliffe Goods Station Branch Junction) gave access to the goods depot. The engineering work involved in laying the 40-acre, 400-wagon yard

Below: **Beighton and Killamarsh.** *S. R. Batty*

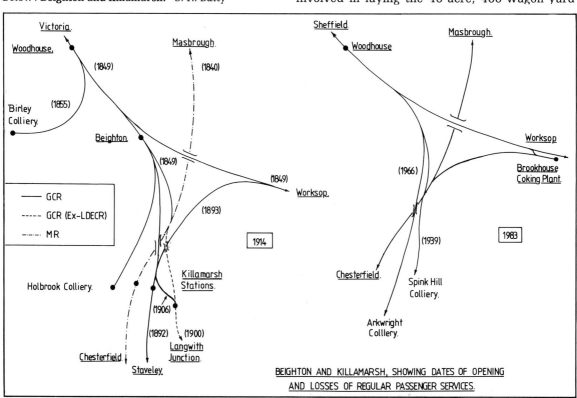

BEIGHTON AND KILLAMARSH, SHOWING DATES OF OPENING AND LOSSES OF REGULAR PASSENGER SERVICES.

Above: **A general view of the western end of Bridgehouses goods yard about 1900.**
Sheffield City Library

Left: **Draymen at Bridgehouses, 1893.**
J. Quick collection

and its 5/8-mile branch was enormous. The River Don was diverted, and 40,000cu yd of spoil removed from there went towards the 250,000cu yd required to raise the site by 10-15ft. Two girder bridges were required to cross Newhall Road and Brightside Lane, and two 25ft spans crossed Sanderson's mill race. A total of seven bridges crossed existing roads. The two-storey goods depot was approached from three directions — Faraday Road, Princess Street and Stevenson Road. The latter ran through the depot, which also had a passenger platform for possible future use. Loads of up to 35ton could be handled by a steam-powered overhead travelling crane supplied by Booth's of Leeds, and smaller items were dealt with by hydraulic cranes from Jessop & Appleby of Leicester.

LDECR passenger services between Sheffield and the east consisted initially of six trains daily each way between Langwith Junction and Pond Street, calling at all stations except Treeton and Woodhouse Mill. (These two stations were served from September 1901.) Locomotives and rolling stock were all of LDECR origin. From July 1903 the Midland started its own service of four trains daily each way between Pond Street and Mansfield, using its own motive power to haul LDECR coaching stock. In direct competition with the GCR, it introduced a Sheffield-London service conveying a through Manchester-Harwich carriage. Departure eastwards was at 16.05, and at 12.53 for Manchester. Patronage was poor, and the service did not survive.

By the end of 1904 the SDR directors could see that the line would never live up to its once hoped for profitability. The large volume of goods traffic eagerly anticipated prior to 1900 had not appeared, and passenger traffic was very low. In the following year attempts were made to tempt the Great Northern Railway into buying it out, but to no avail. The GER was not interested, as its

Left: Ivatt Class 2 2-6-0 No 46402 climbs towards Heeley with a Hope Valley local during the last days of steam in Sheffield. The burrowing approach of the down London line can be clearly seen. *L. A. Nixon*

Below: An interesting 1966 panorama. 'Peak' No D82 leaves Midland station with the 08.07 Bradford (Forster Square)-St Pancras and passes the 'Farm', former railway offices which by this time had been made redundant by the new Sheaf House. The down London line can be seen on the left, climbing to regain a normal level at Queens Road. *B. Stephenson*

traffic had not reached high levels and its running powers to Sheffield were guaranteed, regardless of changes in ownership. An offer was then made by the GCR (as the MSLR became known after completion of the 'Extension') which was acceptable to the LDECR, and the transfer of ownership took place from 1 January 1907.

The years around the turn of the century saw the GCR making improvements made necessary by the vast amounts of traffic created after the opening of its Marylebone main line, whilst the Midland invested money partly because of traffic demands and partly because of yet more public pressure for improvement, as in the 1860s. Wicker goods station had been improved in 1875, but no less than £100,000 was spent there during 1892. The MR offices at Savile Street consisted of three levels of electrically-lit floorspace above a 5,500sq yd bonded warehouse, and in 1892 a new depot for handling timber, stone, coal and bricks was opened at Upwell Street. In 1898 the city's MR customers told the company that the requirements of the town were not being met, and stated bluntly that a much better service was being given to 'lesser towns such as Bradford and Leicester'. In reply, the Midland Chairman, Sir Ernest Paget, said that investment of over £800,000 was planned for the area, of which £216,000 was to be spent on Pond Street station. Proposals had been made at various times to build a joint station for use by the MSLR/GCR and Midland companies, but the engineering difficulties involved had always ruled out such plans. It is doubtful if the Midland even took these ideas seriously. Tied up with the SDR connections, £62,000 was spent at Beighton and Treeton and a further £33,000 at Brightside.

The MR's biggest problem was the bottleneck

Right: **Pond Street station frontage in the early 1900s, with plenty of evidence of the horse age.**
Sheffield City Library

Below: **Ex-LMSR Class 5 4-6-0 No 5088 forges uphill through Millhouses & Ecclesall with a Leeds-Bristol express in July 1948.**
H. C. Casserley

south of Pond Street. Twenty coal trains per day came from the Barnsley line alone, and the climb to Dore & Totley was jammed with traffic. Widening of the entire length was decided upon, with the original twin tracks being given over to Manchester trains and a new double line being built alongside, to the east. A burrowing junction near Queens Road goods depot would allow London traffic to use the main line platforms on the western side of Pond Street. The work was let in two contracts; No 1 from the north end of the station to Havelock Bridge, Heeley, and No 2 from there on to Dore & Totley. Both were taken by C J. Wills. Around the station more arches over the Sheaf were built, to provide more room for extensions of the permanent way, and the tunnel south of the station was opened out after the land had been bought from the Duke of Norfolk. This entailed using 50,000cu yd of brick and masonry

and removing 200,000cu yd of spoil. Island platforms were provided at Heeley, Mill Houses & Ecclesall, Beauchief & Abbeydale and also Dore & Totley. Many bridges were removed completely, and the widening was completed by 1902.

The new station was not completed until 1905. Charles Trubshawe designed the stone-arcaded frontage, but it attracted criticism due to its low appearance and lack of a tower — 'a splendid opportunity lost', to quote the *Sheffield Telegraph*. But the facilities for travellers left little room for complaint. A 300ft awning covered the front of the building where cabs, passengers and luggage entered the premises. The main feature of the rebuilding was the provision of two new through platforms and two new bays (Platforms 3 and 4) by extending the station westwards. The 1870 frontage became Platform 2, which faced the new 1,000ft × 30ft Platform 1. This backed onto

Right: GCR 0-4-4T No 1148B on pilot duties at Victoria. Built by Kitson's of Leeds for the LDECR in 1897, she became part of the GCR establishment after absorption in 1907. *Real Photos*

Below: 'Improved Director' class 'D11' 4-4-0 No 62663 *Prince Albert* awaits a vacant platform for arrival with the 12.03 (SO) Chesterfield (Central)-Sheffield (Victoria) in September 1958. Blast Lane goods depot is on the left. *K. R. Pirt*

several new offices facing out to Sheaf Street, whilst the original offices were demolished to make room for the new bays, Nos 3 and 4. Platform 5 was the original No 1, Platform 6 was a through line and No 7 was a short bay for southbound locals. The easternmost line entered from the south along Platform 9, but about two-thirds of the distance along the station the platform was cut away to the west and renumbered Platform 8. Points gave access to this, but the original alignment continued northwards to the station exit. Four passenger footbridges and two for luggage and mails were provided. Five signal-boxes controlled the station and approaches, including one placed within the station at the meeting of Platforms 8 and 9. A typical winter's day would involve handling about 250 trains, with many more during the summer months. A

newcomer arrived at Pond Street in October 1905, when the Hull & Barnsley Railway started a service between Sheffield and Hull (Cannon Street) via Cudworth. Four trains ran in each direction, covering the distance in a creditable 100min. Apart from a nine-month break in 1908, the trains continued until January 1917, when wartime cuts claimed the service.

Across at Victoria the GCR tracks were quietly choking under the extra traffic generated by the new Marylebone line. The GNR could take some of the blame, though. Since 1873 it had run through services from King's Cross to Liverpool and from 1883 Manchester in $4\frac{1}{2}$hr. Motive power was changed over between MSLR/GCR and GNR locomotives at Grantham. When the Marylebone services started in April 1899 this facility was withdrawn, and GNR locomotives worked throughout. In order to buy off GNR opposition to the London 'Extension' the MSLR had offered to maintain these running powers over Woodhead, and hence the GNR set up a competitive service which added to the general chaos. (The GNR trains disappeared in 1916.) To ease the pressure, widening work was undertaken. This involved realigning Sussex Street to allow extension of the arches below the station, and so permit a new goods line to be laid north of the station. The old goods line became a 290yd platform. At each end of the station the down main line was revised and the bay platforms lengthened. Eastwards from Victoria, several important modifications were

made, with widening being done through to Woodburn Junction, from Darnall to Handsworth Tunnel (at a cost of £33,585) and from the tunnel exit to Woodhouse (£45,052). These schemes were approved in 1900, and created a four-track approach to Victoria which was very effectively bottlenecked by the twin-track 374yd Handsworth Tunnel. Accordingly this was opened up and widened during 1912/3 at a cost of £70,000 by Robert McAlpine & Sons. Further work entailed putting in loops at Darnall and Woodhouse, and eventually traffic problems between Victoria and Woodhouse were greatly eased. Bridgehouses Tunnel east of the goods

Above: **The Sheffield end of Darnall Tunnel, about 1911. This clearly shows the two-track bottleneck created by the bore.** *H. Clayton*

Left: **A slightly later view of the same location, with opening-out well under way.** *Sheffield City Library*

depot was opened out during 1909 to allow two more shunting necks to be installed. Expenditure on the fabric of Victoria took place in a piecemeal fashion, small improvements being made over the years. A new frontage and subway were built in 1908, but funds were low and little favourable comment was attracted. Whereas the Midland had not provided any clock tower at Pond Street, the GCR did manage a rather low, unseemly effort at its station. Fortunately, the Royal Victoria Hotel lent a rather more dignified air to the station's prospect.

These early years of the century saw the development of the Great Central cross-country timetables into a truly dazzling service. The driving force was the Chairman, Sam Fay, who realised that the company had to provide better services than its rivals in order to gain a decent share of the market. He was the first railwayman to recognise the value of good publicity, and all the new services were well advertised as they appeared. The GCR Marylebone main line was regarded by its competitors as an intruder, a latecomer which should be squeezed out if at all possible. The GCR responded with vigour, and embarked on producing excellent services not just to London, but to all destinations which could be reached by means of running agreements with companies to the north, south, east and west. By

the nature of its geographical position, Sheffield was at the very centre of these developments.

In 1900 a restaurant car express was started from Newcastle and Sunderland, in the heart of NER territory, and worked down to Southampton and Bournemouth over LSWR metals. The South of England benefited further from October 1903 with the introduction of a Manchester-Dover

WEEK DAYS.

	a					c						d						d	b					c				e			
LONDON (M'bone) ..dep.		2 45		8 45			10 10 0						1215						3 15	4 30				6 20							
Leicester (Cen.) .... „																			4 35				8 16							
Nottingham (Vic.).. „		4 45		8 15		11 4												5 7				8 43		1135						
Sheffield (Vic.)....arr.		5 15	8 28		8 52		1137											5 9	5 56	12 8										
Sheffield (Vic.)....dep.		5 50	8 go	8 36	9 59		1052 1233 1240											5 17	11 8	12 8	30 9	8 39	9 48	9 53					
Huddersfield ....arr.				10 16			12 8	1 41										5 27				1020			1132					
Halifax .... „				9 44														6 27							12 0					
Bradford (Exch.).. „				10 52			1 8	2 20										5 46				11 7								
Manchester (Cen.).. „				11 9			1215	2 21										6 31				1149								
Manchester (L.R.).. „				10 15			1 37	2 0										7 29				1123								
Stockport (Tiv. D.).. „				9 46			1 50											7 42				1150								
Warrington (Cen.).. „				1032			2 15											7 10				1155								
Southport (Lord St.) „				1222			2147											9 15				1220								
Liverpool (Cen.) .... „				1035			1215																							

	a						c				d				d			h		c				
Liverpool (Cen.) ....dep.		5 10																	6 50		9 30			
Southport (Lord St.) „				7 50		1630													6 55		9 55			
Warrington (Cen.).. „		5 48		8 59		1055													6 55		9 1117			
Stockport (Tiv. D.).. „		6 14		9 46		1053													6 26					
Manchester (L.R.).. „		6 20		9 10		1110 1230 1245					2 50		3 40		5 0				6 55		1025			
Manchester (Cen.).. „		6 57		9 25		1125 12 0					2 18		4 30			7 20				1025 1055			
Bradford (Exchange) „		5 56		9 28		1155									5 0									
Halifax .... „		5 50		9 45		1140									5 27									
Huddersfield ...... „		6 32		10 33		1236									5 19									
Sheffield (Vic.)....arr.		7 35	9 31 1040	1116 1238					4 55			6 23												
Sheffield (Vic.)....dep.	5 35	7 8	9 41 1027	1121 1244					5 46			7 29												
Nottingham (Vic.).. „	7 22	8 20		1212 112					6 18			9 55												
Leicester (Cen.) .... „	8 12	8 57	1055	1244 2					7 41 1045															
LONDON (M'bone) .. „	1025 1155	12 5 1 30	3 0	5 45			6 43			8 39														

SUNDAYS.

	a	m		m	p	m	p	m	p	m
LONDON (M'bone) ..dep.					1115				5 30	
Leicester (Cen.) .... „			8 0	1 26	4 48		7 43		
Nottingham (Vic.).. „			8 55	2 2	5 18		8 17		
Sheffield (Vic.)....arr.			1037	5 9		9 8		
Sheffield (Vic.)....dep.	1 48	2 53	6 40 12 0	152 58 4	57 25 9	3 9 15		
Huddersfield ......arr.		9 2		7 54		1024		
Halifax .... „		10 0		9 27		1347		
Bradford (Exchange) „		10 30		10 0		11 5		
Manchester (Cen.).. „	4 12	8 45 1055 1055		
Manchester (L.R.).. „	3 5	8 45 1 37 3 20 4 10 5 50 9 40 1015 1025		
Stockport (Tiv. Dale) „	4 5	5 54 10 52 3 53		7 34		1029		
Warrington (Cen.).. „	4 37	4 37 11 18 2 5		6 20		1057		
Southport (Lord St.) „	1057 1057	3 253 2 5		1025		
Liverpool (Central).. „	5 5	5 12 10 2 45		6 47		1135		

	a	m	a	m	a	m	p	m	p	m	d	p	m
Liverpool (Central) ..dep.	7 45 1040*		3 50 4 30 6 30		
Southport (Lord St.) „	9 0		2 0		
Warrington (Cen.).. „	8 40 1118*		4 14 4 57 7 18		
Stockport (Tiv. Dale) „	9 30		4 45		
Manchester (L.R.).. „	6 50 1040	1235 4	0 4 55	8 30		
Manchester (Cen.).. „	9 25 12 5	2 40 4 25 5 35 8 45		
Bradford (Exchange) „		1 28	6 15		
Halifax .... „	7 35		5 6	6 45		
Huddersfield ...... „	8 35 1211 1 27 4 25 5 36 1 16 38 1029		
Sheffield (Vic.)....arr.	8 59 1211 1 27 4 25 5 36 1 16 38 1029		
Sheffield (Vic.)....dep.	9 50	1 50	6 43		
Nottingham (Vic.)..arr.	1040	2 43	7 34		
Leicester (Cen.) .... „	1114	3 19	8 3		
LONDON (M'bone) .. „	2 28	5 30	1015		

service via Banbury, Oxford, Reading and Guildford. Departures left Manchester at 09.20 and Dover at 11.22. From July a return nonstop Marylebone-Sheffield service was started, taking 3hr 10min for the up journey and 2min less coming down. These times were both reduced to 3hr dead from October, and reduced again to 2hr 57min from July 1904. At the same time the service was extended to Manchester, and also included a slip portion for Penistone. These 'Sheffield Specials' reached their zenith during the summer of 1905, when 7min were shaved off the Sheffield time to provide the fastest ever journey between the cities, a record that was to stand for many years. The down train left Marylebone at 15.25 and initially consisted of only three coaches hauled by a 4-4-0, although the graceful Atlantics were later used when a slip coach for Leicester was added.

Through carriages were worked between the West Riding and Bristol from 1904, but it was 1906 before the next round of new trains appeared. These started in February with the 09.50 Victoria-Cardiff (arr 15.42) and a return working leaving at 12.25 and giving a Sheffield arrival of 18.30. The attack on South Wales continued in May with a 'Luncheon Corridor Express' departing from York at 11.40 and arriving at Cardiff at 18.14, the return train leaving at 10.10 to arrive at York by 16.35. A through carriage to and from Newcastle was attached, and the coaching stock was provided by the GCR and GWR on alternate days. The same year saw the introduction of the 'Continental Boat Express' from Manchester to Grimsby, where the GCR had excellent docking facilities for its fleet of North Sea steamers. The eastbound train left Manchester

(Central) at 16.22 on Tuesdays, Thursdays and Saturdays and called at Victoria (17.31) and Retford (18.03). The Sheffield stop gave a connection with the 13.40 ex-Marylebone, whilst travellers from as far afield as Edinburgh could connect at Retford. Return journeys giving similar connections were made on Wednesdays, Fridays and Sundays. From April 1909 these trains were extended to Liverpool.

Few Sheffield passengers must have used the Newcastle-Bournemouth service for in 1907 the call at Victoria was deleted and the trains routed via Darnall and Attercliffe, so avoiding reversal in the station. From July 1909 through coaches between Hull and Barry were attached at Victoria to the 11.40 York-Cardiff, and the summer services saw trains to Blackpool, Southampton, Bournemouth, Dover, Cardiff, Barry, Swansea, Bristol, Exeter and Ilfracombe. By April 1910 Victoria was handling over 200 passenger trains daily of all descriptions, from the Marylebone flyers and cross-country marathons to the more humble medium-distance trains and local stoppers. On weekdays the first arrival from Marylebone was at 01.40, whilst the 02.45 departure from London (famous as the 'Newspaper' in later years) arrived, after some smart running, at 06.04. The 08.45 Marylebone-Liverpool gave a connection with a Belfast boat and called at Victoria at 12.28. Trains for Manchester called at 13.32 and 16.01, and dining cars were to be seen on the 16.30 Marylebone-Manchester (Victoria 20.08) and 18.20 Liverpool train calling at 21.34. In the up direction, departures for Marylebone took place at 07.08 (slow), 08.50 (dining car with carriages from Liverpool), 09.36 (through carriages from Liverpool and the West Riding, and dining car from Liverpool) and 11.21 (from Manchester, with a carriage for Bournemouth). The afternoon services began with the 14.15 dining car express from Manchester-Marylebone, followed by the 15.20 from London Road at 16.55. The last two up trains were the 16.00 ex-Liverpool (18.21-25) and the 22.25 ex-London Road (23.54).

The Great Northern Railway provided three trains daily each way between Victoria and King's Cross. A through portion was taken by the 11.00 Liverpool-Cleethorpes and detached at Victoria at 13.42 before being taken onwards by the GNR at 13.50. The other two up trains left Manchester at 15.40 (with dining car) and 22.55, pausing at Victoria at 16.44-48 and 00.25 respectively. Down trains left King's Cross at 12.30 for Sheffield (arr 16.16), and for

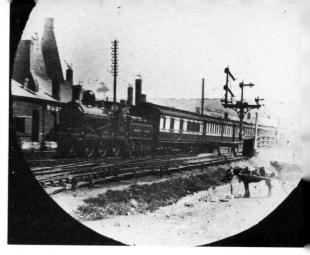

Above: **An LYR 0-6-0 climbs through Wadsley Bridge with the West Riding portion of a down Marylebone dining car express about 1905. The horse is also taking refreshment.** *H. Clayton collection*

Manchester at 18.05 (arr Victoria 21.05 with dining car) and 22.45 (Victoria 02.44-02.53).

Services between Hull and Liverpool consisted of four eastbound and three westbound trains daily, with a fourth west bound terminating at Manchester. A separate Hull and Sheffield service gave three trains from Hull and two return workings. The 14.55 Hull (Paragon)-Manchester (Central) connected at Victoria with the 15.40 King's Cross express, and the 10.30 Liverpool-Hull brought a through carriage from Manchester for Yarmouth, which went forward at 13.00. A connection to Harwich was made by the 13.43 Hull departure with the 14.30 Liverpool-Harwich and Grimsby, which sent its two portions on from Victoria at 16.37 and 16.32 respectively. The numerous local services ran to Chesterfield, Nottingham, Lincoln, Retford, Cleethorpes, Doncaster and Barnsley. Weekends and market days would produce extra trains to Doncaster (via Rotherham and Masbrough), Chesterfield, Penistone, Barnetby and, believe it or not, Tibshelf!

The Midland's day at Pond Street started with the passage of the southbound expresses from Scotland to St Pancras. On Mondays only the 21.15 Glasgow-St Pancras sleeper paused between 03.32 and 03.35, soon to be followed at 03.47-03.50 by the 15.30 ex-Aberdeen corridor. During the remaining days of the week this last train was started from Edinburgh and called at Sheffield from 03.53-04.02, whilst the 23.00 departure from Glasgow followed the ex-NMR route from Masbrough to Beighton. Four London expresses departed during the morning, the first

PENISTONE, BARNSLEY, AND DONCASTER.

WEEK DAYS.	am	am	am	am	am	am	am b	am Saturdays only	am	am	am Saturdays only	am	pm	pm	pm	pm Saturdays only	pm Saturdays only	pm	pm	pm Saturdays only	pm	pm a	pm	pm	pm	pm a	pm	pm	pm Saturdays only	pm	pm a	SUNDAYS. am	pm	pm	pm
PENISTONE ..dep.	....	....	....	7 22	8 20	9 25	....		..	....		11 0	....	1 12	....	....	....	3 10	....	....	3 52	4 47	5 17	6 0	....	....	8 27	....		1035	1145	8 40	2 0	6 5	9 45
Silkstone .... ,,	....	....	....	7 30	8 28	9 33	....		..	....		11 8	....	1 20	....	....	....	3 18	....	....	4 0	4 54	5 25	6 8	....	....	8 35	....		1043	1153	8 48	2 8	6 13	9 53
Dodworth	....	....	....	7 34	8 32	9 37	....		..	....		1112	....	1 24	....	....	....	3 22	....	....	4 4	4 58	5 29	6 12	....	....	8 39	....		1047	1157	8 52	2 12	6 17	9 57
Summer Lane .... ,,	....	....	....	7 42	8 40	9 45	....		..	....		1117	....	1 30	....			3 30	....	....	4 12	5 5	5 36	6 20	....	....	8 46	....		1055	12 3	9 0	2 20	6 25	10 5
Barnsley .... arr.	....	....	....	7 45	8 43	9 48	....		..	....		1120	....	1 3[illegible]	....			3 33	....		4 15	5 8	5 39	6 23	....	....	8 49	....		1058	12 8	9 3	2 23	6 28	10 8
(Court House) dep.	....	....	....	7 47	—	—	9 52	1015	1032	....		1122	....	1 3[illegible]	....			3 35	....		4 17	—	5 41	6 24	7 52	8 35	8 52	....	1045	11 0	1210	9 4	—	6 30	1010
Stairf't (for Ardsley) ,,	....	....	....	7 54	....	....	9 58	1021	1038	....		1127	....	1 40	....			3 41	....		4 23	....	5 47	6 30	7 58	8 41	8 58	....	1051	11 6	1216	9 10	....	6 36	1016
Wombwell .... ,,	....	....	....	8 0	....	....	10 3	1028	1045	....		1132	....	1 45	....			3 48	....		4 29	....	5 53	6 37	8 3	8 48	9 4	....	1057	1113	1223	9 17	....	6 43	1023
Wath-on-Dearne .. ,,	....	....	....	8 6	....	a m	10 9	1034	1051	....		1137	....	1 50	....			3 54	....		4 35	p m	5 59	6 43	—	8 54	9 10	....	11 3	1119	1229	9 23	....	6 49	1029
Mexbro' .... ,,	6 0	7 30	7 50	8 17	....	10 8	1015	1041	1056	1113	1129	1144	1 8	1 56	2 1	3 25	3 52	3 59	4 15	4 35	4 45	5 34	6 6	6 50	9 0	9 2	9 17	1041	11 9	1124	1237	9 30	....	6 56	1034
Conisbro' .... ,,	6 7	7 36	7 57	8 25	....	1016	1021	1049	....	....	1136	1151	....	2 2	2 8	3 32	3 59	—	4 23	4 42	4 52	5 41	6 12	6 58	9 8	—	9 23	1048	—	—	—	9 38	....	7 4	—
DONCASTER arr.	6 16	7 46	8 7	8 34	....	1025	1030	1058	....	1125	1145	12 0	1 20	2 10	2 18	3 41	4 8	....	4 32	4 51	5 1	5 50	6 21	7 8	9 18	....	9 32	1057	....	....	....	9 47	....	7 13	....

	am	am	am	am	am Saturdays only	am	am	am	am	am	am Saturdays only	am	pm Saturdays only	pm	pm Saturdays only	pm	pm	pm	pm b	pm Saturdays only	pm	pm	pm Saturdays only	pm	pm	pm	pm a	pm Saturdays only	pm	SUNDAYS. am	am	pm	pm	pm
DONCASTER ....dep.	..	....	7 35	8 10	....	8 43	8 55	9 53	....	1123	1132	1143	1255	1 40	2 0	3 0	3 20	3 56	4 18	5 20	5 40	6 28	....	7 10	....	8 20	9 31		11 35	....	1055	1215	....	7 55
Conisbro' .... ,,	..	....	7 44	8 21	....	8 52	9 3	10 3	....	1133	1142	....	1 5	1 50	2 10	3 10	3 30	4 6	4 27	5 30	5 50	6 38	....	7 20	....	8 30	9 41		11 45	....	11 5	1225	....	8 5
Mexbro' .... ,,	525	....	7 57	8 27	8 45	8 58	9 15	10 9	1013	1140	1149	1156	1 15	2 10	2 16	3 17	3 41	4 34	4 32	5 38	6 0	6 45	....	7 28	....	8 40	9 50		11a52	6 13	1113	1231	....	8 13
Wath-on-Dearne ...... ,,	531	....	8 2		8 51	—	9 21		1019	1146	—	—	—	2 16	—	3 23	—	4 40		5 43	6 6	—	....	7 34	....	8 46	9 56		11a58	6 19	1119	—	....	8 18
Wombwell .... ,,	538	....	8 8		8 58	....	9 27		1026	1153		....		2 23		3 30	....	4 47		5 50	6 13	....	6 54	7 41	8 15	8 53	10 3		12a 5	6 26	1126	....	....	8 25
Stairfoot (for Ardsley).. ,,	547	....	8 15		9 7	....	9 36		1035	12 2		....		2 32		3 39	....	4 56	....	5 59	6 22	....	7 2	7 51	8 23	9 2	1012		12a14	6 35	1135	....	....	8 34
Barnsley .... arr.	554	....	8 21	....	9 14	....	9 42	....	1042	12 9		....		2 39		3 46	....	5 3	....	6 6	6 29	....	7 9	7 58	8 30	9 9	1019		12a21	6 42	1142	....	....	8 41
(Court House) dep.	556	7 15	8 22	....	—	....	9 44	....	1044	1211		....		2 41		3 48	....	5 4	....	—	6 31	....	—	8 0	—	9 11	•	9 50	—	6 44	1225	....	4 25	8 43
Summer Lane. .... ,,	6 0	7 19	8 26	....		....	9 48	....	1048	1215		....		2 45		3 52	....	....	....		6 35	....		8 4	....	9 15	....	9 54	....	6 48	1229	....	4 29	8 47
Dodworth .... ,,	6 6	7 25	8 32	....		....	9 54	....	1054	1221		....		2 51	....	3 58	....	5 10	....		6 41	....		8 10	....	9 21	....	10 0	....	6 54	1235	....	4 35	8 53
Silkstone .... ,,	612	7 31	8 38	....		....	10 0	....	11 0	1227	....	....	....	2 57	....	4 4	....	5 16	....		6 47	....		8 16	....	9 27	....	10 6	....	7 0	1241	....	4 41	8 59
PENISTONE ...... arr.	620	7 39	8 47	....		....	10 8	....	11 8	1235	....	....	....	3 5	....	4 12	....	5 24	....		6 55	....		8 24	....	9 35	....	1014	....	7 8	1249	....	4 49	9 7

a Saturdays only. **b** Thursdays only.

BARNSLEY, WAKEFIELD, AND LEEDS.

Court House,	WEEK DAYS. am	am	pm	pm	pm	pm Saturdays only	pm	pm Saturdays only		SUND'YS pm	pm	
BARNSLEY ....dep.	8 16	1125	1 56	4 35	6 35	8 5	9 40	1135	....	1225	7 10	....
Stairfoot .... ,,	....	....	....	....	....	....	....	....	....	1235	7 20	....
Staincross(fr Mapplwil),,	8 25	1135	2 7	4 45	6 46	8 16	9 50	1146	....	1244	7 29	....
Notton and Royston.. ,,	8 29	1139	2 13	4 51	6 52	8 22	9 54	1152	....	1250	7 35	....
Ryhill .... ,,	8 34	1144	2 19	4 56	6 57	8 27	9 59	1157	....	1254	7 39	....
								a m				
Harepark and Crofton ,,	8 39	1148	2 25	5 2	7 2	8 33	10 4	12 3	....	1 1	7 48	....
Sandal .... ,,	8 43	1152	2 30	5 6	7 7	8 38	10 9	12 8	....	1 5	7 52	....
Wakefield(W'stgte)arr.	8 46	1156	2 35	5 10	7 11	8 42	1012	1211	..	1 9	7 56	....
Holbeck .... ,,	9 18	1231	3 10	5‖53	7 33	9 33	1045	—	..	1 43	8 37	....
LEEDS (Central) .. ,,	9 22	1234	3 13	5‖57	7 37	9 35	1049	....	....	1 47	8 41	....

‖ Saturdays excepted.

	WEEK DAYS. am	am	pm	pm	pm Saturdays only	pm	pm	pm Saturdays only	pm Saturdays only	SUND'YS pm	pm	
LEEDS (Central) ..dep.	7 10	9 0	1217	2 55		5 5	7 30	8 12	9 40	1 10	8 7	....
Holbeck .... ,,	7 13	9 4	1220	2 59		5 8	7 33	8 15	9 43	1 14	8 10	....
Wakefield (Westgte),	7 37	9 34	1258	3 23		5 35	8 5	9 12	1023	1 40	9 20	....
Sandal .... ,,	7 41	9 38	1 3	3 27		5 40	8 9	9 17	1027	1 44	9 24	....
Harepark and Crofton ,,	7 45	9 43	1 8	3 31		5 46	8 14	9 22	1033	1 49	9 29	....
Ryhill .... ,,	7 52	9 49	1 14	3 38		5 51	8 21	9 28	1041	1 55	9 35	....
Notton and Royston.. ,,	7 56	9 53	1 18	3 42	5 40	5 55	8 25	9 32	1047	1 59	9 39	....
Staincross(fr Mapplwil),,	8 1	10 0	1 24	3 48	5 50	6 0	8 30	9 37	1053	2 4	9 44	....
Stairfoot .... ,,	....	....	....	....	....	....	....	....	....	2 18	9 58	....
BARNSL'Y(Ct.H.)arr.	8 10	1012	1 34	3 58	6 0	6 10	8 40	9 47	11 5	2 24	10 4	....

SHEFFIELD, RETFORD, LINCOLN, GAINSBORO', GRIMSBY (Town), AND CLEETHORPES.

	WEEK DAYS. am Mondays excepted	am		am	am		am	am	am	am	am	pm	pm	pm	pm	pm	pm	pm d Tues., Thurs., & Sats. only	pm	pm	pm	pm	pm	pm	pm	pm	SUNDAYS. am	am	pm	pm	pm
SHEFFLD (V.) dep.	1225	3 0	520	6 55	7 38	818	8 55	9 41	1050	1125	1155	1 0	1 50	2 5	3 33	432	4 37	5 31	5 35	5 52	6 15	a	....	7 55	9 45	11 0	1225	9 35	1 40	6 20	6 50
Darnall (for Hdswth),,		....	..	7 1	....	..	9 1	....	....	1131	....	1 6	....	....	3 39	..	....		....	5 58	....		....	8 1	9 51	....	....	9 41	....	....	6 56
Woodhouse .... ,		....	..	7 8	....	..	9 8	9 53	....	1138	....	1 13	....	....	3 46	..	....		....	6 5	....		....	8 8	9 58	....	r	9 48	....	....	7 3
Waleswood .... ,		....	..	7 13	....	..	9 13	9 58	....	1143	....	1 18	....	....	3 51	..	....		....	6 10	....		....	8 13	10 3	....	....	9 53	....	....	7 8
Kiveton Park...... ,,		....	..	7 21	7 55	..	9 21	10 4	..	1151	....	1 26	....	....	3 59	..	....		5 52	6 18	....		....	8 21	1011	1113	....	10 1	....	....	7 16
Shireoaks......... ,,		....	..	7 26	....		9 26	1010	..	1156	....	1 31	....	....	4 4	..	....		5 57	6 23	....		....	8 27	1016	1123	....	10 6	....	....	7 21
Worksop........ ,,	1248	3 28	..	7 32	8 5	839	9 32	1016	1118	12 1	1219	1 37	2 11	2 27	4 12	..	5 2		6 2	6 27	6 39	7 1	7 14	8 34	1022	1130	1248	1011	2 9	6 48	7 25
Checker House.... ,,	....	....	..	7 39	....	..	9 40	.	....	12 9	....	1 44	—	b	4 19	..	....		6 10	—	....	....	7 22	8 43	1029	....	....	1019	....	....	7 34
RETFORD...... arr.	1259	3 40	..	7 47	8 16	850	9 48	1027	1130	1217	1230	1 51	....	2 38	4 29	..	5 13	6 1	6 18	....	6 49	....	7 32	8 52	1037	1141	1259	1027	2 20	7 0	7 42
Lincoln........ ,,	—	....	..	8 15	9 25	—	1032	....	1157	1 10	—	2 20	....	3 33	5 17	529	....	....	—	....	8 18	....	8 18	—	....	—	—	1135	3 5	....	8 37
Gainsboro'.... ,,	....	4 1	.	....	8 58	..	—	1050	—	1244	....	....	....	3 7	—	—	5 34	....	....	....	....	7 27	—	....	11 7	‖	....	1053	3 3	8 10	8 10
Grimsby(Town) ,,	....	5 5	822	....	1017	..	....	12 5	..	2 12	....	....	....	4 25	....	..	6 32	7 12	....	....	....	8 21	....	....	—	....	....	1217	3 56	9 34	9 34
Cleethorpes .. ,,	....	5 53	837	....	1032	..	....	1220	....	2 27	....	....	....	4 40	....	..	6 55	....	....	....	....	8 36	....	....	....	....	....	1232	4 13	9 49	9 49

	am Mondays excepted	am	am	am	am	am	am	am	am	am	pm	pm	pm	pm	pm	pm	pm	pm	pm	pm	pm	pm	am	am	pm	pm	pm
Cleethorpes...... dep.	....	....	6 30	....	....	....	7 45	....	....	1030	....	[illegible]	....	....	....	2 30	....	4 10	....	5 45	6 45	....	....	8 45	....	4 15	6 35
Grimsby (Town) .. ,,	....	....	6 50	....	....	....	8 7	....	....	1055	....	[illegible]	....	....	....	2 52	....	4 30	....	6 5	7 5	....	....	9 5	....	4 32	6 55
Gainsboro'........ ,,	....	....	7 38	....	....	....	9 23	....	....	1221	....	2 26	....	....	....	4 1	....	5 52	....	....	8 32	....	....	1022	....	5 54	7 45
Lincoln .... ,,	....	....	6 45	6 45	7 55	....	9 20	....	1110	1230	1230	....	....	2 47	....	3 17	4 8	....	6 0	....	8 20	....	....	9 35	1 45	5 25	....
RETFORD........... ,,	2 8	6 5	7 55	8 0	8 24	8 37	1010	1053	1139	1 15	1 20	....	2 50	....	3 41	4 35	4 58	6 25	7 3	....	9 5	9 40	2 8	1049	3 20	6 24	8 23
Checker House .... ,,	....	6 13	....	8 8	....	8 45	....	11 1	....	....	1 28	....	2 58	....	....	....	5 6	6 33	....	....	....	9 48	....	1057	....	6 32	....
Worksop .... ,,	2 20	6 23	8 8	8 15	8 37	8 53	1024	11 8	1152	1 28	1 38	2 53	3 6	3 26	3 54	4 51	5 15	6 43	7 17	....	9 19	10 0	2 20	11 4	3 35	6 39	8 36
Shireoaks............ ,,		6 28	....	8 20	....	8 58	....	1113	....	m	1 43		3 11	....	....	....	5 20	6 48	7 22	....	....	10 5	....	11 9	....	6 44	....
Kiveton Park......... ,,		6 36	....	8 28	....	9 6	....	1121	12 3	m	1 52		3 19	....	....	....	5 23	6 56	7 30	....	....	1013	....	1117	....	6 52	....
Waleswood .... ,,		6 43	....	8 35	....	9 13	....	1128	....	....	1 59		3 25	....	....	....	5 35	7 3	....	....	....	1020	....	1124	....	6 59	....
Woodhouse .... ,,		6 47	....	8 39	....	9 17	....	1132	....	....	2 3	....	3 30	....	....	....	5 39	7 7	....	....	....	1024	....	1128	....	7 3	....
Darnall (for Handsworth),,		6 54	....	8 46	....	9 24	....	1139	....	....	2 10	a	3 37	....	....	....	5 45	7 14	....	....	....	1031	....	1135	....	7 10	....
SHEFFIELD (Vic.) arr.	2 44	6 59	8 31	8 51	9 0	9 29	1047	1144	1221	1 55	2 15	....	3 42	[illegible] 49	4 16	5 14	5 50	7 19	7 45	9 10	9 43	1036	2 44	1140	3 58	7 15	8 59

a Passengers change at Worksop. **b** Stops to set down Passengers from Sheffield or beyond on notice being given to the Guard at Sheffield. **d** Runs from May 7th, 1910, to September 29th, 1910. **m** Stops when required to take up Passengers for Penistone or beyond on notice being given at the Station. **r** Stops at Woodhouse to take up Passengers. ‖ Saturdays only.

SHEFFIELD, ROTHERHAM, WAKEFIELD, AND LEEDS.

WEEK DAYS.	am	am a	am a	am	am	pm	pm	pm	pm
SHEFFIELD (Victoria)....dep.	6 22	7 22	8 0	8 33	10 7	1 58	5 18	6 30	9 40
Attercliffe .... ,,	6 27	7 27	b	8 38	....	....	5 23	....	....
Broughton Lane .... ,,	6 30	7 30	b	8 41	....	....	5 26	....	....
Tinsley .... ,,	6 33	7 33	b	8 44	....	....	5 29	....	....
Rotherham and Masboro' .... ,,	6 42	7 40	8 12	8 52	1022	2 11	5 37	6 42	9 51
Swinton .... ,,	....	7 51	....	9 5	b	....	5 47	b	....
Hemsworth .... ,,	7 11	....	....	9 25	....	2 40	6 9	d	d
Wakefield (Westgate) ......arr.	7 20	8 30	8 50	9 34	11 3	2 51	6 21	7 15	1028
Holbeck .... ,,	7 36	—	9 18	9 51	1122	3 10	6 38	7 33	1045
LEEDS (Central)........... ,,	7 41	....	9 22	9 54	1126	3 13	6 42	7 37	1049

WEEK DAYS.	am	am	am	pm	pm	pm	pm
LEEDS (Central)...........dep.	8 8	9 48	1133	2 41	4 48	7 5	9 40
Holbeck .... ,,	8 11	9 51	1136	2 44	4 51	7 8	9 43
Wakefield (Westgate) ...... ,,	8 28	10 9	1151	3 0	5 7	7 24	10 1
Hemsworth .... ,,	8 39	f	f	....	5 18	f	....
Swinton .... ,,	....	1036	....	c	5 38	....	h
Rotherham and Masboro' .... ,,	9 6	1046	1223	3 34	5 48	8 2	1043
Tinsley .... ,,	....	1052	....	c	5 54	8 8	....
Broughton Lane .... ,,	....	....	1233	c	....	....	....
SHEFFIELD (Victoria)....arr.	9 16	11 0	1240	3 45	6 2	8 15	1053

a Wednesdays only. **b** Stops when required to take up Passengers for Wakefield on notice being given at the Station. **c** Stops on Wednesdays when required to set down Passengers from Wakefield on notice being given to the Guard at Wakefield. **d** Stops when required to set down Passengers on notice being given to the Guard at Rotherham and Masboro'. **f** Stops when required to take up Passengers for Rotherham and Masboro' or beyond on notice being given at the Station. **h** Stops when required to set down Passengers from Wakefield or beyond on notice being given to the Guard at Wakefield.

Above: **Some of the GCR Sheffield, Leeds and Cleethorpes services, October 1909.** *D. Pearce collection*

leaving at 07.20. The Heysham-St Pancras boat train collected portions from Bradford and Halifax and connected with a local arrival from Barnsley before departure at 09.02. Leeds sent its first express at 08.22, which slipped a coach at Masbrough before leaving Sheffield at 09.27. A dining car express followed at 11.08, bringing a portion from Harrogate and taking coaches for Dover, Deal and Folkestone. Further Leeds-St Pancras expresses departed at 12.20 and 14.00, with up trains from Glasgow departing at 16.58 and 19.22 after having carriages attached from Bradford and Halifax. These four up trains all conveyed dining cars, but not so the last London train of the day, the 23.29 departure formed by the 18.44 from Heysham.

Down arrivals on the St Pancras line began at 04.25 with the 00.05 departure for Carlisle, the 'North Express'. The 05.00 St Pancras-Leeds arrived at 08.50 after a creditable run along the Midland main, but the 05.30 from St Pancras took until 11.18 to find its weary way north on the journey to Bradford. These times from London were very modest, and could only be called slow when compared to the lightweight GCR 'Sheffield Specials'. Another Leeds train followed at 12.00, and the first down 'Scotch', the 09.30 ex-St Pancras, called at 12.53 to detach the West Riding through coaches. The 11.30 'Scotch' diner bypassed the city altogether, running via Masbrough. Afternoon St Pancras-Leeds trains arrived at 13.57, 15.50 (with dining car), 17.47 (coaches from Dover, Deal and Folkestone), 18.45 and 20.20 (both diners). Down Glasgow trains mostly went via the 'Old Road', the 11.30 ex-St Pancras taking a Harrogate coach and the 21.30 and midnight trains carrying sleeping cars. The 13.30 down 'Scotch' left a Bradford and Halifax portion at 16.35, and the last down express, the 20.15 St Pancras-Stranraer called at 23.40. Services between Sheffield and Halifax and Bradford worked over the MR's new Royston-Thornhill line, opened in July 1909 and worked mostly with LYR motive power.

An interesting middle-distance service was provided to Hull, with the Midland and North Eastern sending two trains in each direction daily (departures from Pond Street at 09.42 and 17.10), arrivals at 11.23 and 17.19) on a journey time of approximately 1hr 45min. The Hull & Barnsley Railway ran a competitive service into Pond Street which took slightly longer (1hr 55min, best from Cannon Steet), but sending three trains each way. Arrivals were at 11.45, 17.03 and 18.55 and departures at 14.03, 18.58 and 20.28.

Above: **Conversation piece at Midland station, December 1964.** *L. A. Nixon*

Above right: **Canklow 'B1' No 61334 makes a smoky departure for the Hope Valley with a Manchester train on 11 June 1963.** *Ian Slater*

Right: **A St Pancras express heads for Bradway Tunnel behind Class 45 No 90 on 3 May 1970.** *P. J. Rose*

The Northeast-Southwest services used the NER/MR joint line from Wath Road Junction to Burton Salmon, usually known as the Swinton & Knottingley joint line. (This had been opened in 1879 to provide a faster route to York by avoiding heavy congestion at Normanton.) Local departures for York left at 07.05 and 08.18 (having started from Dore & Totley), 09.13, 18.39 and 20.33. Newcastle trains left at 11.25, 13.40 (09.45 ex-Bristol) and 16.47. Three stopping trains to Bristol left each morning at 04.27, 06.07 and 08.00, with Newcastle-Bristol trains calling at 13.28 and 18.12. The use of slip coaches at Masbrough was not confined to the 'Scotches' — the 13.28 arrival served Rotherham in this way, whilst the 12.55 Bristol-York travelled via the NMR line with a through Southampton-Sheffield coach which was cast off at 17.05 before being ferried down to Pond Street. Further arrivals from Bristol took place at 16.20 (with carriages from Bournemouth to York, Leeds and Bradford), 18.30 (carriages from Torquay to Leeds), and 21.40 (the 16.52 Bristol-Leeds).

The Hope Valley route to Chinley, Stockport,

Manchester and Liverpool saw 32 trains each day during April 1910, starting with a departure at 06.22 for Edale which then returned to Pond Street by 08.18. Four trains daily ran each way between Liverpool, Manchester and Sheffield, the Liverpool portions being attached or detached at Chinley. A further service operated from Manchester (Central), sending 14 trains daily over the Hope Valley.

Some of the local passenger stations had undergone at least one renaming by the end of 1914. The original Abbey Houses station of 1870 on the Chesterfield line was renamed Beauchieff & Abbey Dale in May 1874, was slightly altered to

Beauchief & Abbey Dale in December 1889, and finally rechristened Beauchief on 9 March 1914. The next station down the line was the 1870 halt at Ecclesall, renamed Ecclesall & Mill Houses in December 1871 and then changed again to Mill Houses & Ecclesall in May 1884. The SDR station at Tinsley Road became West Tinsley from July 1907, and Meadow Hall was altered to Meadow Hall & Wincobank from July 1899.

The network of private sidings and colliery lines around Sheffield in the years leading up to the Grouping of 1923 was staggering. Although the Midland and Great Central companies generally duplicated each other's sidings, the

Left: **A down Class 9 freight passes Woodhouse behind Darnall '04/1' No 63658.** *J. H. Turner*

Below: **A Tinsley landscape. Class 47 No 47.368 passes the works of T. W. Ward & Son near Broughton Lane with a ballast train in October 1976.** *L. A. Nixon*

Right: **Wicker goods yard, August 1962.** *P. C. H. Robinson*

Left: **'4F' 0-6-0 No 43863 heads south with a coal train along the Midland main line at Beighton. In the background can be seen the ex-LDECR line from Killamarsh.** *B. R. Goodlad*

lion's share of this work fell to the GCR. The original 1855 line at Birley colliery had been extended to a 2mile 1,100yd-branch by 1914, and other systems had grown up at Stocksbridge steelworks (1mile 1,474yd), Holbrook colliery, Beighton (1mile 68yd), Tinsley Park colliery (1,653yd), Dixon's paper mill at Oughtybridge (1,276yd), Beighton colliery (1,162yd) and Tinsley steelworks (718yd). From West Tinsley branches led to the steelwork of Henry Cooper & Co, Edgar Allen, Cooke's, Firth's, and Hadfield's. Access to some of these was difficult, and strict instructions were laid down for movement over the branches. Hadfield's sidings totalled seven in all, two operated by the GCR, two by the MR, two for rubbish and one used only by the steelworks. An incline of 1 in 40 led into the sidings and eight full wagons or 10 empties at 5mph was the maximum load allowed. Firth's branch was not quite so difficult, but the first six wagons had to be braked. Control of train movements was varied at different locations, with, for example, the one-engine-in-steam principle being used on Cooke's siding. Points were sometimes padlocked when the relevant signalbox was out of use, and any shunting then required was conditional upon the loco crew being able to find the padlock key in the signalbox, as at Cooper's and Allen's sidings.

The signalboxes at Attercliffe Junction and Tinsley East could claim the dubious distinction of being amongst the 40-odd boxes on the entire GCR system not to have crossovers provided between the running lines. Having reached the main lines with large loads of coal or steel, further problems were usually encountered by trains heading along the former MSLR main line in either direction. Banking locomotives would be needed from Tinsley station to assist trains to either Darnall or Woodburn, both being approached on steep, tightly-curving lines. From Darnall, eastbound trains were often split for the three-mile climb at 1 in 115 to Kiveton Park. Westbound traffic faced the long slog up to Woodhead, nearly 20 miles away and climbing solidly at 1 in 100-160 all the way. Banking was often necessary, and was officially confirmed from either Woodhouse or Sheffield No 6 box (at the east end of Victoria) to Dunford No 1. The entire stretch from Dunford No 5 box to Darnall Tunnel box was the responsibility of one inspector from the Manchester District Superintendent's Office. Despite having so much of the Sheffield area under his control, the Superintendent had no responsibility for the District Railway. This came under the Staveley inspector, due no doubt to the LDECR origins of this by now rather unloved little system. The Sheffield Goods Manager was in charge of traffic throughout the Northern District of the GCR, from Penistone to Beighton, Barnetby and Torksey, whilst the Engineer's Department was the largest outside the London area, covering Neepsend-Woodhouse East-Killamarsh-Mexborough-Worsbrough, and also the Chesterfield Canal!

On the Midland system the most difficult line to operate was the link to the GCR via Spital Hill Tunnel. The original S&R line to Wicker left the new (1870) line at Grimesthorpe Junction, and the Spital Hill line turned southwestwards away from the approach to Wicker at Tunnel Line Junction. The branch was worked on a train-staff system, and shunters and guards were specially appointed for working the line. Midland traffic was worked less than half a mile from Tunnel Line Junction to the changeover point with the GCR at the summit just beyond the short tunnel, but the gradient within the bore was 1 in 36. This severely limited loads over the line, and a maximum of 17 mineral wagons or 20 vehicles was imposed. These trains were propelled at a maximum of 12mph from the elevated signalbox at a point roughly halfway along the branch from Grimesthorpe. The loads had to be reduced during bad weather to avoid trains stalling on the climb. If a train had to set back and restart, the guard had to check all couplings before any further attempts were made.

Interchange traffic was never very heavy, and the branch was closed during World War 2 to allow explosives to be stored in the tunnel. Reopening took place after the war ended, but the line was finally closed during 1948.

By 1923, traffic on the MR/GCR connection at Nunnery was almost nonexistent, only the occasional train being propelled to the colliery from the Midland's Nunnery Colliery Branch Junction, just over a quarter of a mile from Pond Street. The guard unlocked points to the sidings as necessary. Midland working notices for the area stated that propelling of trains should only be done when two brake vans were available, at least one of which was to be leading. This was regularly done between Holmes Junction and Rotherham with a maximum of 25 wagons, and between Wicker Goods and Grimesthorpe.

Below: **The Nunnery area, 1923.**
S. R. Batty/P. C. H. Robinson

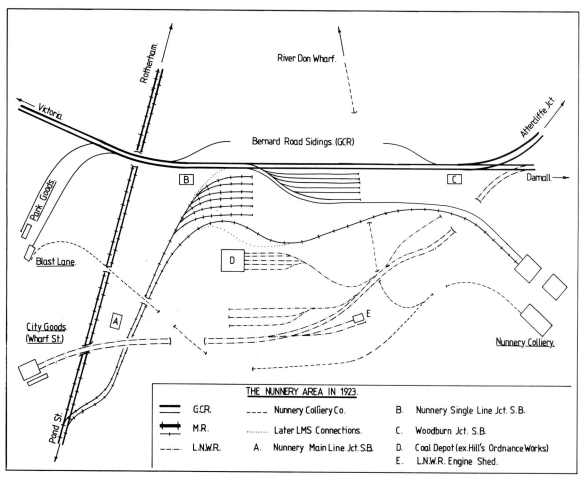

THE NUNNERY AREA IN 1923.

GCR.	Nunnery Colliery Co.	B. Nunnery Single Line Jct. S.B.
M.R.	Later LMS Connections.	C. Woodburn Jct. S.B.
L.N.W.R.	A. Nunnery Main Line Jct. S.B.	D. Coal Depot (ex. Hill's Ordnance Works)
		E. L.N.W.R. Engine Shed.

3 1923-1947 — Post-Grouping Scene

The Grouping of 1923 resulted in all former Midland Railway lines being taken over by the London Midland & Scottish Railway, and the Great Central Railway system going to the London & North Eastern Railway. One curious outcome was that the former District Railway became an LNER line connected at both ends to the LMSR system. Several years were to pass without any significant changes being made to the fabric of the new railway system, but the services, which had been so badly savaged during the last years of World War 1, were quickly improved to try and approach some of the best 1914 services.

The fastest time to London was still being achieved on the Marylebone route, with the 15.20 departure from Victoria (the former 'Sheffield Special') taking 3hr 10min instead of the prewar best of 2hr 50min. Stops were included at Leicester and Nottingham, with a Penistone halt being inserted on the forward run to London Road. Motive power was usually an ex-GCR

'Director' 4-4-0 throughout, but later in LNER days the train was lengthened to seven bogies (including one for Bradford) and the new 'B17' 4-6-0s were then used. The service remained in the timetable until 1939.

King's Cross trains had disappeared from 1916, but the service was resumed in June 1924 when a Pullman service was started, following the LNER's success with the 'Harrogate Pullman'. The 'Sheffield Pullman' left King's Cross at 11.05 and ran over ex-GNR metals to Nottingham,

Below: **The crowded western end of Victoria in early LNER days. The '04' is heading towards Woodhead with a coal train, passing two pilot locos standing near the entrance to Bridgehouses goods depot. The ex-GCR 4-4-0 is setting back with a single wagon, probably removed from the train standing in the bottom right-hand corner of the scene.** *Ian Allan Library*

Above: **'Improved Director' No 5502** *Zeebrugge* **at Victoria. Behind, an ex-GNR Class C1 Atlantic receives attention before the next duty.** *P. Holmes collection*

where a 4min stop was allowed. From here ex-GCR lines took the train to Victoria, arrival being at 14.20. The time of 3hr 15min was reasonable for a journey two miles longer than the pure GCR route, and of course including the Nottingham stop. The up train left Victoria at 16.45, called at Nottingham at 17.38 and arrived in King's Cross at 20.00. On the inaugural service of 2 June, five Pullman cars conveyed 22 first class and 130 second class passengers who had paid supplementary fares of 6s (30p) and 3s 6d ($17\frac{1}{2}$p) respectively. Included in the passengers were four heads of the Pullman Co and seven representatives of the LNER, all of whom were taken on a tour of Firth & Sons' steelworks during the stopover. During regular service the train was hauled by a selected few locomotives — GNR Atlantic No 4426 and GCR 4-6-0s No 425 *City of Manchester*, No 1164 *Earl Beatty* and 'Director' No 437 *Prince George*. Sadly, the train attracted very little custom, and only one month after introduction the service was retimed and its

running order reversed. The up train left Victoria at 10.30 and the return service departed from King's Cross at 18.05, and from April 1925 the Nottingham stop was removed and the train extended to run to Manchester. From Victoria the train ran via Retford to London in 2hr 57min, equalling the best GCR time in 1914, but still the 'Pullman' failed to generate sufficient traffic. In autumn 1925 the train was cancelled, and the Pullman put to work on the 11.10 King's Cross-Leeds and Bradford 'West Riding Pullman'.

The LMSR was not to be outdone, however. In March 1925 a return St Pancras-Sheffield-Bradford service was introduced, unofficially known as the 'Yorkshireman'. The up train left Bradford at 09.55 and the down St Pancras at 16.55, both trains placing Sheffield within 3hr 10min of the capital, including a Leicester stop. Revenue was considerably better than that produced by the LNER Pullman, and from October 1937 a second train was put on. The Leicester stop was removed and the times between St Pancras and Pond Street came down to 2hr 52min. This didn't last long though — the Leicester halt was reinstated in 1939 and the time increased to 3hr 5min mainly because even the new Jubilee 4-6-0s were overtaxed. Both trains disappeared for ever in September 1939.

Right: **An eastbound stopper leaves Victoria behind 'Director' class 'D10' No 5437** *Prince George* **on 14 September 1929. Originally named** *Charles Stuart Wortley,* **No 437 was renamed after the monarch's youngest son in 1920.**
W. L. Good

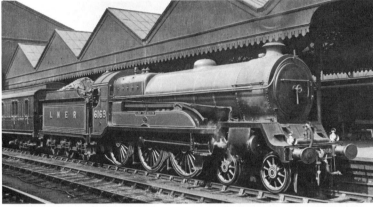

Left: **The GCR Class 9P 4-6-0s were reclassified 'B3' by the LNER. No 6169** *Lord Faringdon* **stands at Victoria with a Cleethorpes train about 1935.**
T. G. Hepburn/Rail Archive Stephenson

Left: **Gresley 'D49/3' 4-4-0 No 327** *Nottinghamshire* **on a Hull slow train at Victoria in 1935.**
T. G. Hepburn/Rail Archive Stephenson

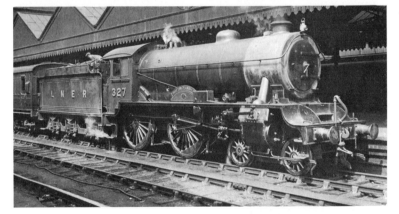

Right: **Gresley 'A1' Pacific No 2547** *Doncaster* **pauses with a King's Cross-Aintree Pullman special for the Grand National on 29 March 1935.**
T. G. Hepburn/Rail Archive Stephenson

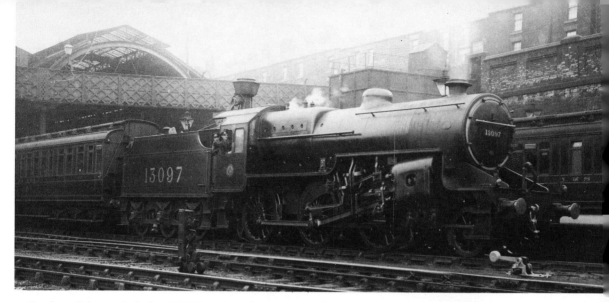

During this period the LMSR created three named trains which served Sheffield well beyond nationalisation and firmly into the BR era, and it is perhaps appropriate at this stage to look at the early history of these services. The Midland line St Pancras morning departure for Edinburgh was set at 09.05 in 1927, and this train was christened the 'Thames-Forth Express'. Fast running was achieved as far as Nottingham, but from here to Sheffield the line was beset with mining subsidence and PW slacks. A Halifax coach was left at Sheffield, and the main train proceeded to Edinburgh via Leeds, the Settle & Carlisle and Waverley route. The up train left Edinburgh at 10.03, and had additional stops at Appleby, Hellifield and Melton Mowbray. Trains were made up to seven coaches and were hauled over LMSR metals by MR/LMSR 4-4-0s until the 'Jubilees' appeared. During World War 2 the down train ran only as far as Sheffield, and without the favour of any title.

The second LMSR titled train of 1927 to grace Sheffield was the 'Thames-Clyde Express', which ran to Glasgow along the ex-GSWR route via Annan, Dumfries, Mauchline and Kilmarnock to St Enoch station. Departure from St Pancras was at 10.00 and the down train ran to Leeds via Chesterfield and Masbrough, missing Pond Street completely. Arrival at St Enoch was at 18.38 after intermediate stops at Kettering, Leicester, Chesterfield, Leeds, Carlisle and the GSWR stations. The up train left Glasgow at 09.30 and ran via Sheffield, eventually reaching St Pancras at 18.25. The diversion via Pond Street slowed the train considerably, due to hard climbing and extra mileage along the Leeds-Chesterfield section. A brief pause was made at Trent to detach a

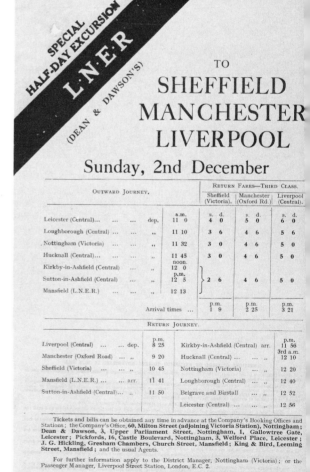

SPECIAL HALF-DAY EXCURSION

L·N·E·R

(DEAN & DAWSON'S)

TO

SHEFFIELD
MANCHESTER
LIVERPOOL

Sunday, 2nd December

OUTWARD JOURNEY.					RETURN FARES—THIRD CLASS.		
					Sheffield (Victoria).	Manchester (Oxford Rd.)	Liverpool (Central)
				a.m.	s. d.	s. d.	s. d.
Leicester (Central)...	...	...	dep.	11 0	4 0	5 0	6 0
Loughborough (Central) ...	...	,,		11 10	3 6	4 6	5 6
Nottingham (Victoria) ...	...	,,		11 32	3 0	4 6	5 0
Hucknall (Central) ...	...	,,		11 45	3 0	4 6	5 0
				noon.			
Kirkby-in-Ashfield (Central)	...	,,		12 0			
				p.m.			
Sutton-in-Ashfield (Central)	...	,,		12 5	} 2 6	4 6	5 0
Mansfield (L.N.E.R.)	...	...	,,	12 13			
		Arrival times ...	,,	p.m. 1 9	p.m. 2 25	p.m. 3 21	

RETURN JOURNEY.							
				p.m.			p.m.
Liverpool (Central) ...	...	dep.	8 25	Kirkby-in-Ashfield (Central)	arr.		11 56
							3rd.a.m.
Manchester (Oxford Road) ...	,,	9 20	Hucknall (Central) ...	...	,,		12 10
Sheffield (Victoria) ...	...	,,	10 45	Nottingham (Victoria) ...	,,		12 20
Mansfield (L.N.E.R.) ...	...	arr.	11 41	Loughborough (Central) ...	,,		12 40
Sutton-in-Ashfield (Central)...	,,	11 50	Belgrave and Birstall ...	,,		12 52
				Leicester (Central) ...	...	,,	12 56

Tickets and bills can be obtained any time in advance at the Company's Booking Offices and Stations; the Company's Office, 60, Milton Street (adjoining Victoria Station), Nottingham; Dean & Dawson, 3, Upper Parliament Street, Nottingham, 1, Gallowtree Gate, Leicester; Pickfords, 16, Castle Boulevard, Nottingham, 3, Welford Place, Leicester; J. G. Hickling, Gresham Chambers, Church Street, Mansfield; King & Bird, Leeming Street, Mansfield; and the usual Agents.

For further information apply to the District Manager, Nottingham (Victoria); or the Passenger Manager, Liverpool Street Station, London, E.C. 2.

For Conditions of Issue see over.

It will assist the Railway Company in making arrangements for your comfort if you TAKE TICKETS IN ADVANCE.

London, November, 1928. (via London Road South Junction) No. 1789.

Harrison & Sons, Ltd., 44-47, St. Martin's Lane, London, W.C. 2. 7,8/0

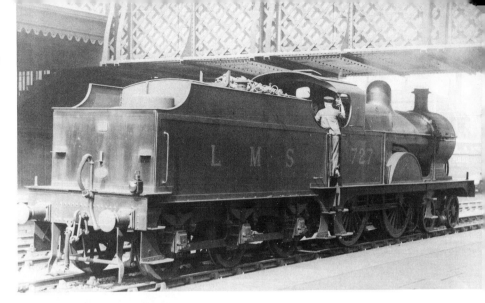

Nottingham portion, but this was taken off in 1937. World War 2 hit the service very heavily, the down train being slowed by no less than 3hr and usually being made up to 14 bogies (hauled by an unassisted 'Royal Scot' 4-6-0) as far as Leeds. The up train was similarly loaded, and slowed by 2hr 45min.

Through trains between the West Riding and the Southwest dated back to Midland Railway days, and in early LMSR years the 'Devonian' was somewhat mistitled, as this third named train of 1927 started life as a Bradford-Bristol service with only three through coaches for Paignton and Torquay. The southbound train left Bradford (Forster Square) at 10.52, reversed at Leeds and arrived at Pond Street at 11.42. Departure at 11.47 was followed by a 53min, nonstop run to Derby, where a Bournemouth coach was dropped and replaced by a Newcastle-Bristol vehicle off the 10.20 departure from York. Fast LMSR running to Bristol was followed by a gentle dawdle along the GWR main line for the three South Devon coaches, which ran through to Kingswear from May to September. The northbound train left Paignton at 09.15, and arrived at Temple Meads at 12.13 where a 22min wait preceded departure on a similar schedule to the southbound train. Sheffield was reached at 16.25.

69

Left: **Millhouses' No 362, a Deeley rebuild of Johnson's Class 2 4-4-0. Note the bogie brakes.** *W. L. Good*

Below: **No 731 was another Millhouses locomotive, seen here in the mid-1930s. These superheated Class 3 engines were built between 1900 and 1905.** *P. Hughes*

Restaurant cars ran between Leeds and Bristol, and 'Jubilee' power was used as soon as the locos became available. Both up and down trains disappeared in September 1939 for the duration of hostilities.

At a more local level, both the LMSR and LNER started to feel the pinch of competition from road transport in their passenger businesses, and in January 1929 they took measures to try and recover some lost ground. Both companies made arrangements with Sheffield Corporation whereby some of the longer bus routes from the city (to Bakewell, Barnsley, Buxton, Chesterfield and Huddersfield) were to be operated by the LMSR and LNER. Shorter distances were to be covered by a joint Corporation/railway scheme, and the local services remained entirely in the hands of the Corporation. Both companies jointly paid £63,000 for this sharing of services, made up of £33,700 for half ownership of 55 existing buses and purchase of 14 new vehicles, plus a goodwill

payment of £29,300. A similar scheme was introduced later in the year when the two companies jointly ran a service of six return bus trips per day to Manchester, this time without any involvement from the Corporation.

The lean years of the late 1920s and early 1930s saw very little change being made in the goods facilities and services. Bridgehouses depot was damaged by fire in July 1924, but the only losses were amongst the documents and papers plus a little water damage to the lower floors, and matters were soon put right for less than £3,000. Nine years later the depot was extended to accommodate a further 26 wagons. A very early casualty was Attercliffe station on the Woodburn-Rotherham line, which closed to passenger and goods traffic from 26 September 1927. On a more positive note, the loops at Woodhouse were extended by threequarters of a mile in 1925, so allowing Grimsby and Lincoln traffic to be worked almost independently of Nottingham and London-

Right: Built primarily to handle fast fish trains from Grimsby, the Class B5 4-6-0s were known throughout their lives as 'Fish Engines'. Lincoln shed's No 5185 leaves Victoria with a Retford stopper on 2 July 1939. *J. P. Wilson*

Centre right: One of Neepsend's 'B2' 4-6-0s, No 5423 *Sir Sam Fay* at Victoria, 4 May 1929. *W. L. Good*

Below: The 13.22 Skegness-Manchester (Piccadilly) passes Handsworth behind Class 40 No 40.090. *A. R. Kaye*

QUORN HUNT STEEPLECHASES
at LOUGHBOROUGH
First Race about 2-0 p.m.　　　Last Race about 4-40 p.m.

Monday, 23rd April
Dean & Dawson's EXCURSION to

LOUGHBOROUGH

FROM	TIMES OF DEPARTURE.		RETURN FARES.	
		Special Express.	1st Class.	3rd Class.
	a.m.	a.m.	s. d.	s. d.
DONCASTER (Central)	9 56	..	14 2	8 6
MEXBORO'	10 10	..	12 8	7 7
ROTHERHAM & MASBORO'	10 21	..	11 6	6 11
SHEFFIELD (Victoria)		10 55	9 10	5 11
CHESTERFIELD (Central)	10 41	..	7 4	4 5
ILKESTON	11 11	..	3 6	2 1
KIMBERLEY	11 21	..	3 6	2 1
BASFORD	11 27	..	3 3	2 0
NOTTINGHAM { Victoria	..	11 55	2 11	1 9
{ Arkwright Street	..	12 0	2 9	1 8
		p.m.		
LOUGHBOROUGH (Central) .. arr.	..	12 19		

Passengers RETURN the SAME DAY ONLY from LOUGHBOROUGH (Central) at 6-15 p.m.

In the event of the Races being either postponed or abandoned this excursion will not run, provided the Company receives notice at the station of departure in sufficient time to cancel the arrangements.

CONDITIONS OF ISSUE OF EXCURSION TICKETS ADVERTISED ON THIS BILL.
These tickets are issued subject to the Conditions of issue of Ordinary Passenger Tickets, where applicable, and also to the following conditions:—

Neither the holder nor any other person shall have any right of action against the Company or any other Railway Company or persons owning, working, or using any railway, vehicles, vessels or premises (whether jointly with the Company or otherwise) upon which such tickets may be available in respect of (a) injury (fatal or otherwise), loss, damage or delay however caused; or (b) loss of or damage or delay to property however caused.

The tickets are available only by the trains specified in the Company's notices.

A ticket which covers the outward and return journey shall not be used for the return journey unless and until the outward journey has been completed.

If a ticket is used in contravention of these conditions, the holder will be required to pay the difference between the sum actually paid for the ticket and the full ordinary return fare between the stations named on such ticket.

The period of availability of these tickets will not be extended, nor will any allowance be made for return portions not used.

Children under three years of age may travel free when accompanied by a fare-paying passenger, children of three years of age and under 12 years of age are conveyed at half-fares, minimum fare one penny.

No luggage allowed on the outward journey excepting small handbags, luncheon baskets, or other small articles intended for the passenger's personal use during the day.

On the return journey passengers will be allowed to take with them free of charge, at their own risk, 120 lbs., First Class, and 60 lbs., Third Class, of goods which they have purchased for their own use. Furniture, linoleum, musical instruments, cycles, mail carts, typewriters, and other similar articles are excepted from this arrangement.

In those cases where the rail journey is not continuous through tickets do not include the cost of conveyance from one station to another in the same town.

PASSENGERS are REQUESTED TO OBTAIN THEIR TICKETS IN ADVANCE.

Tickets and bills can be obtained any time in advance at the Company's Booking Offices and Stations; also from the Company's Offices, 63 Market Place, Sheffield, and 60 Milton Street (adjoining Victoria Station), Nottingham; Messrs. Dean & Dawson Ltd., 57 High Street, Doncaster, 32 Westgate, Rotherham, 42 Fargate, Sheffield, 25 Cavendish Street, Chesterfield, and 2 Upper Parliament Street, Nottingham; Mr. J. W. Dawson, 7 Haymarket, Sheffield; Mr. W. G. Fox, 99 London Road, Sheffield; Mr. T. A. Rose, 36 Firth Park Road, Sheffield; Messrs. Altham Ltd., Sheffield; G.W.R. Office, 68 High Street, Sheffield; Messrs. Pickfords Ltd., 15 Castle Boulevard, Nottingham; and the usual Agents.

For further information apply to the District Manager, Peterboro' or Nottingham; the District Passenger Manager, L.N.E.R., London Road Station, Manchester; or the Passenger Manager, Liverpool Street Station, London, E.C.2.

London, April, 1928.

For a Programme of Holiday Tours write to or call at Dean & Dawson's Offices.

Stafford & Co., Ltd., Printers, Netherfield Nottingham.
140—10,500

LNER

No. 305

Above: **Race special to Loughborough, April 1928.**
D. Pearce collection

Right: **Cleethorpes excursion handbill, November 1928.** *D. Pearce collection*

Extended Holiday Period Excursions
DEAN & DAWSON'S EXCURSION TICKETS TO
BRIGG　GRIMSBY DOCKS
CLEETHORPES
and †LOUTH
SATURDAYS
Commencing 3rd NOVEMBER and until further notice
(22nd December excepted)
For 6 and 15 days

FROM	Times of Departure		RETURN FARES—Third Class.			
			Brigg	Grimsby Docks	Cleethorpes	†Louth
	a.m.	p.m.				
DEEPCAR	10 1	1 39	9/9	12/9	13/6	NB
Oughty Bridge	10 6	1 43	9/3	12/9	13/0	NB
Wadsley Bridge	10 11	1 1	9/0	12/3	12/9	NB
Neepsend	8 30	1 5	8/9	12/0	12/3	NB
SHEFFIELD (Victor.)	11 12	1 58	8/6	11/9	12/3	12/6
Darnall		11 66	8/0	11/3	11/9	NB
Woodhouse	9 50	1 0	7/9	11/0	11/0	NB
Waimwood	9 56	9 12	7/3	10/6	10/9	NB
Kiveton Park	10 4	2 20	6/9	10/0	10/3	10/9
Shireoaks	10 9	2 25	6/3	9/6	9/9	NB
WORKSOP	11 37	1 21	6/0	9/0	9/6	10/0
RETFORD	11 12	2 02	5/0	8/0	8/3	8/9
	p.m.					
GAINSBOROUGH (Central)	12 7	3 16	NB	6/0	6/6	8/0
	a.m.					
Kirton Lindsey	11 13	3 38	NB	5/0	5/0	NB
	p.m.					
Brigg	12 35	3 52	NB	NB	5/0	NB

NB—No bookings

Passengers return the following Saturday or Saturday week, as under:—

From Cleethorpes	From Grimsby Docks	From †Louth	From Brigg	FOR
12 20 p.m.	12 35 p.m.	12 20 p.m.	1 36 p.m.	Shireoaks, Kiveton Park, Waimwood, Woodhouse and Darnall
2 20 p.m.	2 35 p.m.	1 45 p.m.	3 38 p.m.	All other Stations

†—Louth passengers change at Grimsby Town in each direction

PASSENGERS ARE REQUESTED TO OBTAIN THEIR TICKETS IN ADVANCE.

Tickets and bills can be obtained in advance at the Company's Booking Offices and Stations; also at Sheffield from the Company's Office, 63 Market Place; Messrs. Dean & Dawson Ltd., 42 Fargate, Mr. J. W. Dawson, 7 Haymarket, Mr. W. G. Fox, 99 London Road, Mr. T. A. Rose, 36 Firth Park Road, Messrs. G. A. Woodcock Ltd., 43 The Wicker, and Messrs. Altham Ltd.; in Worksop from the Co-operative Society, 16 Eastgate; and the usual Agents.

For further information apply to the District Passenger Manager, L.N.E.R., London Road Station, Manchester; the District Managers, Lincoln and Peterborough; or the Passenger Manager, Liverpool Street Station, London, E.C.2.

FOR CONDITIONS OF ISSUE SEE OVER
For particulars of the Excursions in connection with the CHRISTMAS HOLIDAYS see separate announcements

London, October, 1928.

LNER

No. 1726

Dean & Co. (Stpt) Ltd., Cheadle Heath, nr. Manchester—1394—125/10,500.

bound trains. The up line from Darnall had a new loop installed as far as Woodburn, and a total of £36,000 was spent on improvements at the station, consisting mainly of a new platform. LMSR improvements were equally sparse, with new trackwork being laid in 1936 for empty stock sidings at Heeley (one siding for 10 vehicles), Nunnery (three sidings, 10 vehicles) and Dore & Totley (five sidings, 46 vehicles). During the following year £140,000 was spent on improvements in the handling of coal and steel traffic at Sheffield and Rotherham. Roundwood yard was extended by 437 wagons to a total capacity of

Left: An up goods passes between Darnall MPD and the Cravens railway equipment works behind '04/1' No 6575. *P. Holmes collection*

Below: Less than six months after delivery from North British Locomotive Co at Glasgow, Ipswich 'B17' 4-6-0 No 2806 *Audley End* awaits departure for home from Victoria on 4 May 1929. Note the mountain of coal in the tender. *W. L. Good*

Bottom: An autumn morning at Nunnery in 1958. 'J11' No 64329 propels two carriages from Victoria into the ex-GCR sidings as a BR Standard Class 5 prepares to take empty stock down to Midland station. *K. R. Pirt*

765, whilst Woodhouse Mill yard was increased from 420 wagons capacity to no less than 1,100 on 22 sidings. Queens Road goods depot handled 162,000ton of material in 1936, and was felt to justify expenditure on the renewal of the wooden decking within the building. The year 1932 saw the final renaming of Mill Houses & Ecclesall to Millhouses & Ecclesall on 18 July, a change which probably benefited no one except the LMSR sign-writers.

Undoubtedly the biggest event of the interwar years was the LNER sanctioning of the Manchester-Sheffield-Wath electrification scheme in 1936. This pioneering decision was the culmination of over 20 years of brooding. John G. Robinson, the GCR Locomotive Engineer, had been sufficiently impressed by an American 1,500V dc system he had seen in 1913 to consider seriously the idea for use on the Wath-Woodhead-Manchester line, but other commitments (and a war) had put an end to his thoughts. The LNER drew up a scheme in 1926, but once again the idea was shelved. By the mid-1930s the Sheffield-Manchester line was crammed with traffic ranging from light 250ton expresses to slow, loose-coupled coal trains of 1,100ton or more. The passenger service was restricted by the large number of freight trains, and track capacity could not be extended to give any more flexibility. Woodhead's tunnels were already in a poor state, and the removal of steam traction would greatly ease maintenance problems.

Final approval was given in October 1936, but the initial specifications differed somewhat from the system which finally emerged nearly 20 years later. A total of 88 electric locomotives were to be used to replace 181 steam locomotives, consisting of nine express passenger machines weighing 100ton, 69 mixed traffic locomotives of 80tons and 10 banking locomotives of 75ton. These latter were to be converted from existing locomotives on the Newport-Shildon line in Teeside. Overhead collection of direct current at 1,500V was to be used, the first example of this system to be adopted after its recommendation by the Pringle Committee of 1927 for use in long-distance schemes. All traffic was to be electrically-hauled, the eastern changeover points being new sidings at Woodhouse and Bernard Road for goods trains and Victoria station for passenger traffic. New motive power would require a new motive power depot, and to meet this need a new two-section steam/electric depot was to be built at Darnall, where a new flyover would allow light engine movements between shed and station to keep clear of the main running lines. Steam facilities were to include a 70ft turntable, a 100,000gal water tank and a coaling plant. A total of $74\frac{1}{2}$ route miles (covering 293 single-track miles) would be electrified at a cost of £1.5-2million.

Line speeds were expected to increase from 25 to 35mph for slow passenger trains, from 40 to 50mph for expresses, from 28 to 40mph for express freight and from 15 to 22mph for a 1,000ton coal train. In practical terms this meant that the 10.03 Victoria-London Road, with two intermediate stops, would take $46\frac{1}{2}$min instead of 55min, and the 12.09 Bernard Road-Guide Bridge freight would need only 1hr 29min instead of 2hr 3min. Locomotive mileages were expected to reflect high availability, giving annual figures of 2,550,000 freight loco miles, 950,000 passenger loco miles and 500,000 shunting miles.

Below: **Football excursion handbill, December 1928.** *D. Pearce collection*

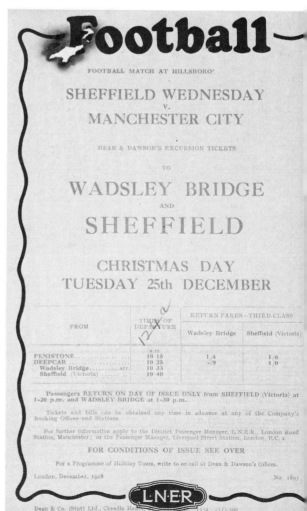

Above: **Still bearing her GCR number, LNER 'D7' 4-4-0 No 705 reposes at Neepsend in July 1924. Built by Kitson's in 1892, she carried a Westinghouse brake pump from 1903 until withdrawal in 1933, one of only two 'D7s' so fitted.** *J. Quick collection*

Left: **Football excursion handbill, April 1936.** *D. Pearce collection*

The first contract for the new works was placed in early 1937, when Henry Lees & Co of Glasgow successfully tendered for construction of the new Darnall coaling plant — a slight touch of irony! Soon afterwards the overhead equipment was contracted to British Insulated Cables, and Metropolitan-Vickers started work on the mixed-traffic locomotives. These were to develop 1,850hp and drive four axles on two articulated bogies, hence having a wheel arrangement of Bo+Bo. The buffing and drawgear was attached directly to the bogies and not to the locomotive underframe. Work went ahead quickly, and an estimated completion date of late 1940 was in sight when war stopped all work. One locomotive (No 6701) had been completed by then and half of the civil engineering finished. Darnall depot was well under way and the flyover had been completed. From the outbreak of war, work on the depot and all existing contracts was completed, but all unstarted work was deferred.

The new Darnall depot came into use during mid-1943, and replaced the previous depot at

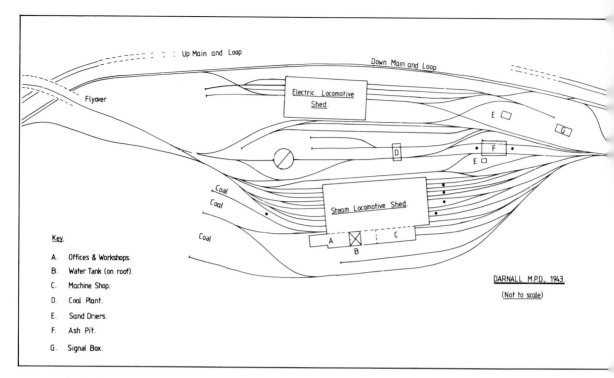

Up Main and Loop

Down Main and Loop

Flyover

Electric Locomotive Shed.

E

G

D

E

F

Coal
Coal

Steam Locomotive Shed.

Coal

A

C

B

DARNALL M.P.D., 1943.

(Not to scale)

Key.

A. Offices & Workshops.
B. Water Tank (on roof).
C. Machine Shop.
D. Coal Plant.
E. Sand Driers.
F. Ash Pit.
G. Signal Box.

Neepsend (where the station had closed on 28 October 1940) which had served the MSLR/GCR/LNER continuously for nearly a century. No precise opening date has come to light, but the Neepsend depot is shown in excellent detail in the MSLR route plans of 1884. After closure the buildings survived until the early 1960s before being completely demolished. The entire depot was placed on the up side of the line between mileposts 40 and 41, east of the station and opposite Sheffield No 1 signalbox. Its turntable could accommodate a wheelbase of 59ft 10in compared to only 55ft 2in of the Victoria table.

A further casualty of 1939 was the former District Railway, which nominally closed from 11 September. Passenger facilities were withdrawn from Catcliffe and West Tinsley, although goods traffic was retained. A brief reopening took place in the winter of 1946/47, but closure soon followed and the goods service was finally withdrawn in October 1960. By the mid-1930s the LMSR had reduced the Sheffield-Mansfield service to three trains daily each way, with one extra train on Saturdays. The motive power continued to reflect the isolated nature of the short line, with an ex-MR Class 2 4-4-0 hauling a pair of LNER coaches for most of the services. Trains left Pond Street at 09.43, 15.24 and 18.22 (plus one at 11.00 on Saturdays) and returned at 11.50, 17.46 and 20.17 (14.01 SO).

Above: **Darnall MPD, 1943.** *S. R. Batty*

Top right: **A prewar view of 'B2' 4-6-0 No 5428** *City of Liverpool* **at Neepsend shed.** *J. H. Turner collection*

Right: **Neepsend 'D9' 4-4-0 No 5110** *King George V.* *W. L. Good*

Below: **A general view of Darnall MPD in BR days.** *Real Photos*

4 1947-1965 —
Electrification and the End of Steam

In September 1947 the LNER gave approval for the electrification to continue. The intervening war years had taken their toll, however, and the cost was revised to £6million with completion at least four years away. One statistic which was produced at the time claimed that the scheme would save 100,000ton of coal per year, which in the austere and fuel-hungry days of postwar Britain must have been intended to sweeten the pill of disappointment somewhat. The major item of expense was the previously unforeseen need to build a new twin-track tunnel at Woodhead, brought about by the dereliction and decay which had overtaken the two single bores.

Electrification progressed in three stages, the first being the Wath-Dunford section where huge loads of coal were being hauled over a very heavily graded stretch of line. This was completed by February 1952, and electrification from London Road up to Woodhead was finished off during June 1954. Thus Sheffield was at the end of the queue, and had to wait until September of that year before reaping the full benefit of the scheme. At a late stage of the work, over 4,000ton of shale collapsed in the Woodhead Tunnel approximately 300yd from the eastern portal, and took six months to clear. The remaining work

between Dunford and Victoria was all but completed by this time, and the collapse was indeed a bitter blow. The tunnel construction was supervised by British Railways Eastern Region, but operation of the line was to be the responsibility of the London Midland.

At Darnall depot (which had by now been servicing steam locomotives only for nearly 10 years) the four-road electric loco shed, which had lain partially completed since 1940, was finished during 1952. Some extensive track modifications were made at the eastern end of Victoria station around No 4 signalbox. During 4/5 December 1948 some 35 crossings were altered, but very few trains were diverted and none cancelled. Further work was done in 1953 when a new 110-lever signalframe was installed in connection with the final resignalling plans. No 3 box, at the west end of Victoria, was removed and replaced by a new, brick-built 60-lever box on the down side of the line just above Wicker. The space so released allowed improvements to be carried out on the up goods line. Resignalling did cause some further expense for the electrification scheme, and

Below: **Sheffield (Victoria) station, 1953.**

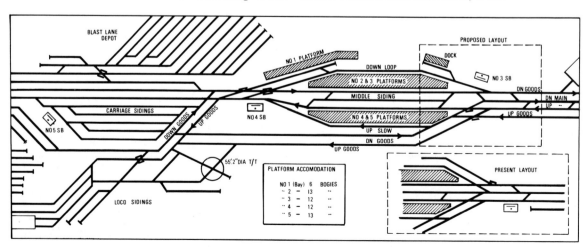

Above: **A Chesterfield-Sheffield (Victoria) local passes Darnall behind a 'C13' 4-4-2T about 1949. The pits for the unfinished electric traction depot can be seen on the right.** *B. N. Collins*

Below: **Victoria on 15 May 1954. Darnall 'B1' No 61169 stands in the centre road whilst 'C13' 4-4-2T No 67439 arrives with empty stock.** *H. B. Priestley*

Bottom: **An eastbound stopper awaits departure behind 'J11' 'Pom-Pom' 0-6-0 No 64292.** *Real Photos*

no mean delay with the completion of work eastwards to Rotherwood. Originally the only semaphore signals which it was intended to replace with colour lights were the distant signals and any whose view to drivers was likely to be obstructed by overhead equipment. When the Wath line was approved for opening, however, the inspecting officer recommended that all signals, except those on the approaches to Manchester, should be so replaced. Line occupation from Victoria to Rotherwood was intense and the work had to be fitted in whenever possible amidst the constant flow of traffic.

Motive power provision had been revised during a cost-cutting exercise shortly after nationalisation, when the mixed-traffic order was reduced to 58 locomotives and a single class of only seven machines was allowed for the express passenger service. These latter were a six-axle Co-Co development of the Bo+Bo locomotives, producing 2,500hp and not having any articulation of the bogies. The buffing and drawgear was attached to the underframe directly, unlike their mixed traffic cousins. Delivery commenced in 1954, in time for No 27000 to take part in the opening ceremony at Victoria on 14 September. A party headed by Sir Brian Robertson, BTC Chairman, travelled from King's Cross via Retford in an eight-coach train hauled by 'A4' Pacific No 60008 *Dwight D. Eisenhower* which gave an excellent nonstop run of 2hr 51min to Victoria. No 27000 then took over and was whistled away by Sir Brian at 11.45 on an easy schedule to London Road, reached at 12.42. On the return trip several passengers lowered the carriage window whilst travelling through the new tunnel and enjoyed the first ever smoke-free passage through Woodhead.

Full public services started with the introduction of the winter timetable on 20 September, when the fastest time across the Woodhead line came down to 51min, achieved by the 13.25 (Mondays only) from London Road. The best time in GCR days had been 50min, but temporary PW slacks at Dunford (15mph) and Penistone (25mph) kept speeds slightly below par. Trains were sent through the tunnel only 5min apart when traffic was heavy, and line capacity was increased by 50%. More coal traffic was expected to follow after the closure of several Lancashire collieries in the near future, and Rotherwood was equipped with a 70ft turntable to assist in dealing with the extra flow of steam-hauled coal trains arriving from the East Midlands. The last section of the electrification work was finally energised in February 1955, when all steam-haulage to Barnsley Junction, Penistone finally ceased.

Within six months the electrified railway was reaping benefits for the Eastern Region. Congestion was greatly reduced, the 65 locomotives spent only 2hr on shed every five days, covering

Below: **Class EM2 No 27002 climbs near Beeley Woods with a special train on 12 September 1954, the day of the official opening of the Sheffield-Manchester electric passenger services.** *B. R. Goodlad*

Below right: **A Class 76 (formerly Class EM1) rattles through Wadsley Bridge with a train of empties in 1980.** *S. R. Batty*

the work previously done by 110 steam locomotives and saving 315 crews. But problems did
occur. The ER's Chief Operating Superintendent,
H. C. Johnson, said that the permanent way was
not up to the new standards of performance available from the locomotives, and that speed restric-
tions were all too frequent. Maximum loads from
Wath were limited to 750ton because of a lack of
braking power, and communication between
drivers of locos at the front and rear of a banked
train was by means of coded blasts on the air
horns — a hark back to steam haulage which was
hardly suited to efficient running. (All these problems were to be overcome in later years.) He also
commented that 40 miles was too small for such a
system and that electrification should be
extended, but this idea fell on stony ground. What
would the protagonists have said if they could
have foreseen the MSW's tragically short, under-
utilised life of barely 25 years?

Apart from the electrification work the early
days of British Railways saw several other
important developments which should not be
overlooked. Uppermost were the efforts to revive
the passenger services along the principal routes
from the city, services which by 1945 had fallen
to a mere shadow of prewar standards. The
'Thames-Forth Express' was restored to a through
Edinburgh service from 1 October 1945, but the
addition of further stops and some decelerations
over the next year combined to give a total
journey time of 10hr 32min. The up train fared
even worse — no less than 11hr 17min was needed
to reach St Pancras after a departure from Edinburgh (Waverley) at 10.10. The winter timetable

of 1950-51 showed journey times of 65-70min for
the $39\frac{1}{2}$ miles to Leeds compared to 48-50min in
1939, and 69-74min for the $38\frac{1}{2}$ miles to Trent,
compared to a previous best of 52min. The 38
miles to Nottingham by the ex-GCR route fared
even worse — no less than a full hour was the
best available time.

Not until 1957 did the fortunes of the 'Thames-
Forth' improve, when at last the train was greatly
accelerated and also renamed as the 'Waverley'.
A fast nonstop run from St Pancras to Nottingham
was rattled off in 123min, and the Carlisle arrival
brought forward by 40min. Edinburgh was
reached (via the Waverley route) at 18.52,
9hr 37min after leaving St Pancras at 09.15. The
up train was similarly treated, but these long
journey times could not compete seriously for
Anglo-Scottish traffic in the face of competition
from the East Coast main line, and the winter
train was soon cut back to an unnamed
St Pancras-Leeds and Bradford service. After
years of haulage by MR/LMSR 4-4-0s, 'Jubilees'
and 'Royal Scots', the diesel era produced Type
45/46 power and more acceleration. Between
Sheffield and Leeds the train followed the Swinton
& Knottingley Railway route between Wath Road
and Moorthorpe after 1967, and finally disappeared in 1969 when the Waverley route itself
was closed.

The 'Thames-Clyde Express' had run
throughout the war, but in October 1945 its Edinburgh portion was replaced by restaurant cars for
the run to Glasgow. It was not until 1949 that the
title was replaced and the train settled down to a
steady time of 10hr 13min going up to St Pancras

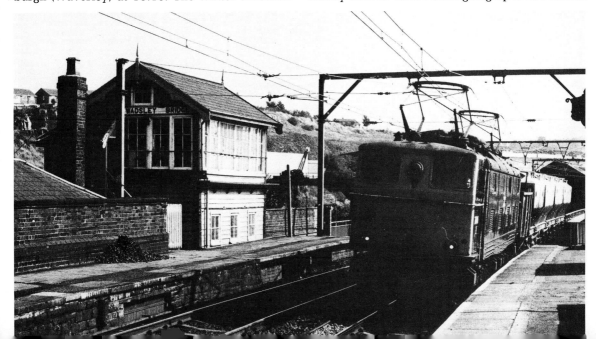

Left: 'B1' 4-6-0 No 61130 crosses the Wicker arches with a Manchester stopping train and passes a new EM2 Co-Co locomotive.
K. Field/Rail Archive Stephenson

Below: A Sheffield (Victoria)-Marylebone express passes Bernard Road sidings on 28 March 1948. The 'B1' 4-6-0 No 1179, is less than a year old. *S. G. Taylor*

Bottom left: Class EM1 Bo+Bo No 26056 *Triton* enters Victoria with an up train of coal empties on 22 July 1963. *B. Stephenson*

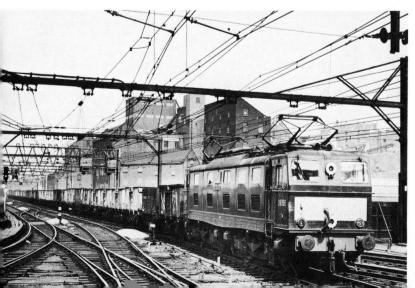

Top right: Tommy visits Victoria on 27 August 1969. After leaving with the 09.45 for Piccadilly . . .

Centre right: . . . the locomotive returned later in the day with a diverted Manchester-London express. These scenes were taken during the last few months of electric passenger working. *Both V. Bamford*

Right: The 'Scotch' expresses were not always powered by 'Jubilee' or 'Royal Scot' 4-6-0s in BR steam days. On 14 June 1958 the down 'Waverley' arrived behind Fowler 2-6-4T No 42373 and Stanier Class 5 No 45253. *P. J. Lynch*

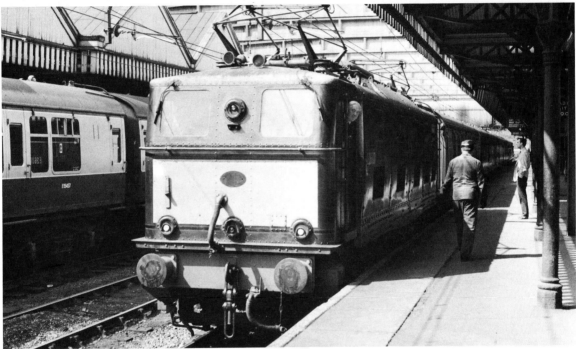

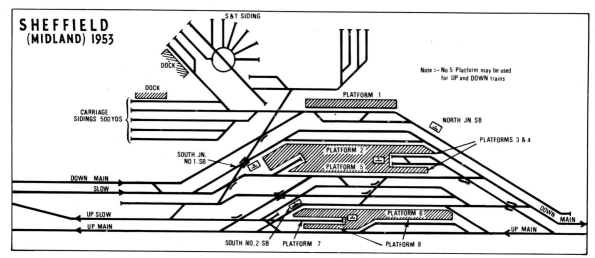

SHEFFIELD (MIDLAND) 1953

S&T SIDING

DOCK

DOCK

CARRIAGE SIDINGS 500 YDS

Note :- No 5 Platform may be used for UP and DOWN trains

PLATFORM 1

NORTH JN. SB

PLATFORMS 3 & 4

SOUTH JN. NO 1. SB

PLATFORM 2

PLATFORM 5

DOWN MAIN

SLOW

UP SLOW

UP MAIN

DOWN MAIN

UP MAIN

PLATFORM 6

SOUTH NO.2 SB   PLATFORM 7   PLATFORM 8

and 8min less for the down train. For several years the train was powered by almost anything that was available, but from 1954 a regular rostering of '6P' and '7P' locomotives improved timekeeping greatly. The down train ran via the NMR route until 1967, when both trains were diverted via the S&K route to Leeds, producing the worst ever Nottingham-Leeds service due to mining subsidence. No less than 71min was required to run from Sheffield to Leeds, compared to only 48min in 1939! When the 'Waverley' was discontinued during the winter months the 'Thames-Clyde' carried an Edinburgh portion as in World War 2. The train's title disappeared in 1975, and the train itself fell by the wayside in

face of WCML competition soon afterwards, long after it had outlived its usefulness as an Anglo-Scottish service.

Returning to the postwar period, 1947 saw the creation of Sheffield's own train to the capital, the 'Master Cutler'. The LNER's prewar 07.30 Victoria-Nottingham-Leicester-Marylebone

Above: **Sheffield (Midland) station, 1953.**

Below: **Southern Region green coaching stock leaves Victoria on the York-Bournemouth train of 13 September 1958 behind 'B1' 4-6-0 No 61152.** *K. R. Pirt*

breakfast car special (arrival time 10.40) had always been popular, and the ER sought to revive this train but with an extra stop at Rugby and a longer journey time. Departure was fixed at 07.35 and Marylebone was eventually reached at 11.25. After a couple of year's running this train was accelerated by 15min, and named 'The Master Cutler' from 6 October 1947, when the then Master Cutler, R. A. Balfour, drove the first train to Marylebone behind 'B1' 4-6-0 No 1223. Despite being a mere shadow of 1939 standards, the train was popular and regularly loaded to 10 or 11 bogies. Poor timekeeping by the Sheffield and Leicester 'B1s' resulted in a 12min deceleration and the down train suffered a similar shuffling of times. Before naming, this train left Marylebone at 18.15 and arrived at 22.14, and was accelerated to a 22.02 arrival at Victoria after naming. This improved to 21.58 during 1949, but fell back to 22.08 in 1953. Restaurant cars were carried, and for a brief spell these were replaced by the ex-Southern Region Bulleid 'Tavern' cars after these had been expelled from their home territory. Howls of protest from the 'Cutler' regular clientele soon led to the reinstatement of the conventional vehicles!

The return of Gresley Pacifics to the ex-GCR lines in 1951 saw the 'Cutler' regularly hauled by an 'A3' locomotive, along with several expresses over Woodhead. Soon afterwards, however, the run-down of the GCR began. By 1958 the title had disappeared from the line, although the train con-

tinued to run for the benefit of Nottingham passengers. The title was transferred to a new, diesel-hauled Pullman train from Victoria to King's Cross via Retford. Departure from Sheffield took place at 07.20, and after a brief call at Retford the train arrived at King's Cross at 10.05. Return times were 19.20 from London and 22.05 arrival in Sheffield. To make the most of the Pullman set, a further return working was fitted in during the day before the down 'Cutler' left at 19.20. This train was never officially named, but was generally known as the 'Sheffield Pullman'. Down departure was at 11.20 with stops at Peterborough, Grantham and Retford, and the up train at 15.20. Both trains covered the distance in 2hr 55min, hauled by the early members of the English Electric 2,000hp Class 40.

Success rapidly followed the new 'Master Cutler' train, which was 52min faster than the former GCR-routed train and 28min faster than the 07.05 departure from Midland station for St Pancras. During the first week of operation 1,200 passengers were carried, and the third week saw customers being turned away. The time of 2hr 45min was thought capable of improve-

Below: '**J11' 0-6-0 No 64329 takes refreshment before hauling the Pullman stock of the 'Master Cutler' from Nunnery sidings to the washing plant on 25 October 1958.** *K. R. Pirt*

ment to 2hr 30min when engineering work on the ECML was finished, but tests made during April 1958 showed that this pace could not be maintained.

Between 1966 and 1968 some juggling of departure times took place, the evening departure from King's Cross being changed to 18.15 for a short period before reversion to 19.20 and a fast 2hr 33min journey down. The up train needed 2hr 35min and the midday 'Pullmans' were altered to leave King's Cross at 10.50 and Victoria at 15.35, taking 2hr 42min and 2hr 45min respectively. Many passengers travelled from Scunthorpe and Doncaster to join the up train, and in the late 1960s this contradicted BR's plans to concentrate all London-Sheffield traffic on the improved Midland line. Consequently the 'Master Cutler' disappeared from GCR/GNR metals from 7 October 1968, when the title was transferred to a Midland non-Pullman departure at 07.15, calling at Leicester and reaching St Pancras at 09.58 after a 2hr 43min run. The return train left at 17.55 and took one minute less. Thus Sheffield lost four Pullman trains, and an excellent service to King's Cross, at one stroke. Use of the 'Cutler' path along the East Coast main line was made by the new 'Hull Pullman' from this time. Acceleration to 2hr 30min was finally achieved during

1972/73, after the train had been diverted to run along the Erewash Valley line, but the 'Cutler' had to wait until October 1982 before the availability of HST sets allowed a further reduction to 2hr 18min up and 2hr 17min down.

Postwar naming of express passenger trains continued with the Bradford (Exchange)-Marylebone 'South Yorkshireman'. The LNER had run a 10.00 departure from Bradford with a return from Marylebone at 18.20, and also had a Sheffield departure at 16.55 reaching Victoria at 20.01. Both services were reflected in the newly-named train which commenced running on 31 May 1948, maintaining the Bradford departure time but leaving Marylebone at 16.55 and reaching Victoria at 20.42, much later than the prewar train. This poor time was due mainly to extra stops at Aylesbury and Chesterfield, and when poor patronage allowed the latter to be cut out the arrival at Victoria was changed to 20.26. This proved too optimistic and the time was soon put back ot 20.40. Loads usually reached 10 bogies, and the down train would leave three coaches plus two restaurant cars at Sheffield before plodding on to Bradford via Penistone and Huddersfield. The up train did not call at Penistone but made conditional stops from Huddersfield before the 11.20 arrival at Victoria. A Low Moor Stanier '5MT' would bring the up train from Bradford (No 5101, in ex-works condition, hauled the first train) and hand over to a Leicester 'B1' for the 11.27 departure for Nottingham, Loughborough, Leicester, Rugby, Aylesbury and Marylebone, reached at 15.30. Such gentle progress during the middle of the day ensured that the up train was always used less than the down service, and during a coal shortage of 1951 the entire train was cancelled for several weeks.

Below: **Even after electrification, the Bradford portion of the 'South Yorkshireman' continued to be steam-hauled. LMR Class 5 No 45101 has arrived at Victoria and is about to hand over to 'A3' Pacific No 60102** *Sir Frederick Banbury* **for the journey to Marylebone.** *R. Hewitt*

Right: 'K3' 2-6-0 No 61964 attracts attention whilst waiting to take over a Manchester-Doncaster train on 4 June 1960. *B. Stephenson*

Below: The 17.00 Bradford (Exchange)-Marylebone enters Victoria behind an unidentified LYR Hughes 'Dreadnought' 4-6-0 in 1935. *T. G. Hepburn/ Rail Archive Stephenson*

Bottom: A Victoria-Nottingham semi-fast passes Beighton behind 'K3/2' 2-6-0 No 61943. *B. R. Goodlad*

The Low Moor Stanier '5MT' which hauled the Bradford portions was usefully employed from Sheffield between trips. After the up 'South Yorkshireman' had departed the loco worked the Newcastle-Bournemouth train forward to Leicester at 12.00. Arrival at Leicester at 13.34 gave ample time to refuel the locomotive before departure at 15.43 with the return working from Bournemouth, reaching Victoria at 17.18. In LNER days the ex-LYR Hughes 4-6-0s had been used on the Bradford-Sheffield leg, but the greater number of Bradford trains ensured a quick return to Low Moor for the visiting locomotive. After electrification the train continued to be steam-hauled between Sheffield and Bradford, as steam/electric changeovers were not made at Penistone. In the winter timetable of 1960 the 'South Yorkshireman' disappeared when the destruction of the ex-GCR began in earnest with the abandonment of the through passenger services north of Nottingham. The vacated paths of the 'Yorkshireman' were roughly taken up by DMU services between Marylebone and Nottingham, Nottingham and Sheffield (Midland), and Sheffield and the West Riding.

Today's Harwich-Manchester service can trace its ancestry back almost 100 years, to 1885 when the Great Eastern Railway began a service from Parkeston Quay to connect with steamers docking from Europe. Unofficially known as the 'North Country Continental', this train ran to York with portions for Birmingham, Manchester and Liverpool and until 1906 was composed entirely of six-wheeled stock. Departure from Harwich was at 07.00, and the two Birmingham coaches were detached at March for collection by the LNWR. At Lincoln the Manchester and Liverpool portions were worked forward by the MSLR/GCR as two separate trains, whilst the main portion (including a dining car) went on to York. The train was suspended during World War 1, but renewed afterwards with the dining car going on to Liverpool. Both the westbound portions were worked as one train, leaving Lincoln at 11.32 and travelling over GCR metals to reach Manchester (Central) at 13.55 and Liverpool (Central) at 14.43. The new 'B17' 4-6-0s were used by the LNER, and the locomotive would work through from Harwich to Manchester, running 216 miles in $5\frac{3}{4}$hr of continuous duty. Coaching stock was well-utilised too; before returning on the next day's up train, a return trip to Hull via Sheffield and Doncaster was fitted in to the schedule. The postwar era saw more changes, with no direct Lincoln-Retford line and the Liverpool and York portions cut out. Leaving Lincoln, the train had to travel northwards along the former GNR/GER joint line to Gainsborough before running back to Retford and Sheffield. After electrification the

Below: 'B17' 4-6-0 No 61627 *Aske Hall* **retires to the bay platform at the western end of Victoria after bringing the down 'Continental' into the station.** *K. Field/Rail Archive Stephenson*

Left: Nocturne. 'B1' No 61055 on station pilot duties at Victoria in the early hours of 4 January 1964.
J. C. Haydon

Below: Diesel power on the Great Central line. The York-Bournemouth leaves Victoria behind Darnall English Electric Type 3 No D6810.
M. S. Eggenton

'Sandringham' 4-6-0 handed the train over to a Co-Co for the run to London Road. Today's service is very much intact, following the original route to March but now running via Peterborough, Grantham, Nottingham and Chesterfield before reaching Sheffield (Midland) prior to departure along the Hope Valley for Manchester Piccadilly). Departure from Parkeston Quay is at 07.18, Midland is called at between 11.42-11.53 and Manchester reached at 12.57. The up train leaves Piccadilly at 15.12, pauses at Sheffield (16.15-16.27) and finally reaches Harwich at 21.10. Together with the remains of the Nottingham-Glasgow service, these trains were diverted from May 1982 to run between Chesterfield and Sheffield via the former NMR route, or 'Old Road'. Leaving Chesterfield and passing Eckington and Beighton the trains then climb up to the former MSLR at Woodhouse and drop into Midland via the Nunnery curve. Southbound trains follow the opposite path, and so all traffic thus avoids the

need to reverse in Midland station before or after negotiating the Hope Valley.

By the time the electrification was completed in early 1955, BR's Modernisation Plan was about to appear. This produced great changes in the Sheffield area, and it is perhaps appropriate at this point to look at various motive power affairs and view an operating system that was to be swept away within the succeeding 10 years. The Midland Railway operated two depots in Sheffield, Grimesthorpe being the oldest. When the Sheffield & Rotherham Railway opened in 1838 it had used a small two-road shed adjacent to the Wicker terminus, but the Midland Railway found this depot to be inadequate. In 1860 a new shed was planned north of Brightside station, and this circular building was constructed by C. Humphreys and opened the following year. Demolition of the Wicker shed took place in 1862. After the opening of the Chesterfield line in 1870 further building took place slightly to the north

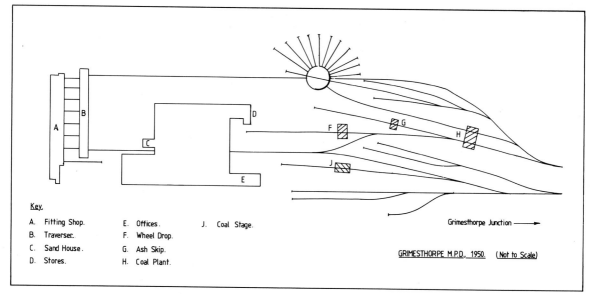

Key.

A. Fitting Shop. E. Offices. J. Coal Stage.
B. Traverser. F. Wheel Drop.
C. Sand House. G. Ash Skip.
D. Stores. H. Coal Plant.

Grimesthorpe Junction ──────▶

GRIMESTHORPE M.P.D., 1950. (Not to Scale)

Above: **Grimesthorpe MPD, 1950.** *S. R. Batty*

and a new shed was opened in 1877, amidst the darkest and gloomiest part of the city. A 46ft turntable was installed within the shed, and an eight-road fitting shop added after 1898. In 1901 a second, outdoor turntable of 60ft (later rebuilt to 65ft) was added, and the original 1861 building was taken out of use. As part of the LMSR's motive power depot improvement scheme, new coal and ash handling facilities were installed by 1937. During MR days the shed had been coded as No 25, and the LMSR gave the depot the code 19A during 1935. Regional changes of 1958 saw the ER take full control of the Sheffield area, and the depot's final code became 41B. The Sheffield area modernisation plan of 1961 required the site to be cleared to make way for a new freight depot, and the shed was offically closed during December of that year. Diesel locomotives made use of the shed as a stabling point for a short while, but demolition was completed by the end of 1962.

The Grimesthorpe allocation always consisted of freight and mixed traffic locomotives, with only a very few passenger classes being present. (At the close of LMSR ownership one such guest was an ex-SDJR '2P' 4-4-0, No 324.) During BR steam days the mainstay of the depot was that ubiquitous workhorse the ex-LMSR '4F' 0-6-0, with a clutch of Stanier '8F' 2-8-0s being provided for the heavier turns. Relics from MR days included Class 1F 0-6-0 tanks and '2F' 0-6-0 tender engines which could trace their ancestry back to the 1870s. Together with a handful of 'Jinty' 0-6-0Ts,

these shunters were employed in the goods yards at Wicker, Queens Road and Brightside. The Queens Road locomotive would return to the depot only at weekends, where a boiler washout and inspection would be administered. Diesel 350hp shunters arrived from 1955, and were stabled in the old repair shop, but the shunters hung on almost to the bitter end.

Passenger locomotives were provided by Millhouses shed, situated between Heeley and Millhouses & Ecclesall stations, on the down side of the line. The eight-road straight shed was opened in 1901, when it was known as Ecclesall and coded 25A as a subshed of Grimesthorpe. The LMSR recoded it 19B in 1935, and the changes of 1958 resulted in the code being changed again to 41C. During LMSR days the allocation consisted mainly of 4-4-0 machines, but these were partially replaced from 1937 by the new 'Jubilee' 4-6-0s. Transfer to the ER from 1958 earmarked one or two locos for early retirement. 'Jubilee' No 45609 disappeared for scrap in 1960 when the ER could not justify the necessary expense to keep such an alien machine alive. Similarly, Millhouses' No 40907 became the Eastern's only Compound 4-4-0, and was quickly reduced to scrap at Doncaster. Seven 'Royal Scot' 4-6-0s were allocated in early 1960, but their stay was cut short by the depot's closure from 1 January 1962, when all the '6Ps' and '7P' 4-6-0s were stored at Barrow Hill or Staveley GC. The 'Jubilees' were then revived and sent to the Manchester area, and the remainder to Canklow or Doncaster. The main shed building still stands today, being used as industrial premises.

Above: Grimesthorpe 'Crab'
No 13138 at home, alongside LMS-
built Compound 4-4-0 No 1091.
W. L. Good

Right: Grimesthorpe shed fitting shop
in July 1920.
National Railway Museum

Below: Prior to the opening of
Tinsley MPD, diesel locomotives
were stabled at Grimesthorpe and
later allocated to Darnall. This early
1960s view shows Brush Type 2 and
English Electric Type 1 motive
power at Grimesthorpe. *IAL*

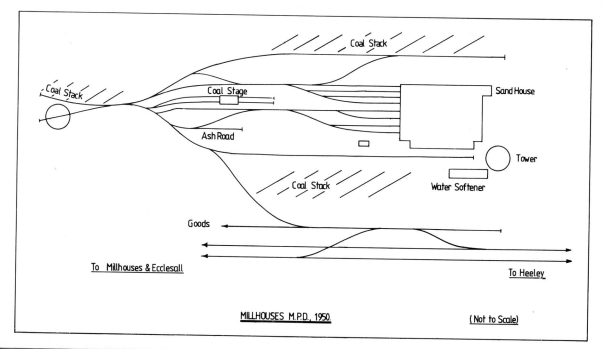

Coal Stack

Coal Stack

Coal Stage

Sand House

Ash Road

Tower

Coal Stack

Water Softener

Goods

To Millhouses & Ecclesall

To Heeley

MILLHOUSES M.P.D., 1950.

(Not to Scale)

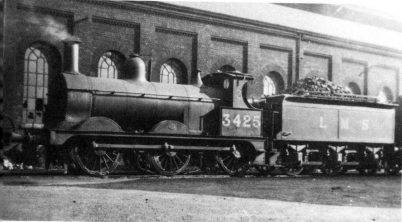

Above: **Millhouses MPD, 1950.**
S. R. Batty

Left: **Johnson Class 2 0-6-0 No 3425 was one of the MR's mass-produced goods engines. Seen at Grimesthorpe in the mid-1930s, still carrying MR boiler fittings and cab.** *P. Hughes*

Below left: **Johnson 2-4-0 No 227 in store at Grimesthorpe in 1932.** *W. L. Good*

Below: **'Jinty' No 16631, a Grimesthorpe locomotive, seen in May 1932 not long after construction.** *W. L. Good*

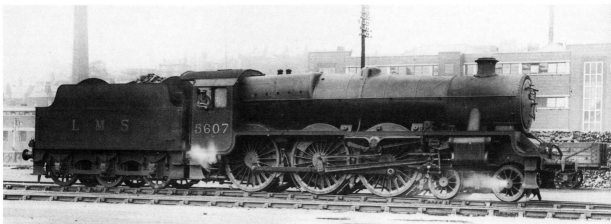

Top: **Millhouses shed in April 1910.** *NRM*

Above: **'Jubilee' No 5607 was just over a year old and still unnamed when photographed at Millhouses in September 1935. It carries the original domeless boiler and is attached to one of the 10 modified Fowler tenders built for the class. This locomotive was later named** *Fiji.* *W. L. Good*

Right: **Front ends at Millhouses — BR Standard '4' 2-6-0 No 76088 and 'Jubilee' 4-6-0s Nos 45615** *Malay States,* **45636** *Uganda* **and 45594** *Bhopal.* *A. Howard Thomas*

Canklow depot was situated 1½ miles south of Masbrough station on the original NMR line. Facilities for locomotives had been available from these early times, but the Canklow Junction depot was not built until 1900 after the MR had spent nearly £28,000 on land, clearance and buildings. The new depot was sub-coded 25B to Grimesthorpe, and was responsible for freight locomotives in the Rotherham area. Reorganisations gave Canklow the codes 19C and 41D from 1935 and 1958 respectively, and the depot became one of the last Eastern Region steam depots from February 1965. Locomotives allocated included '3F' and '4F' 0-6-0s and almost as many Stanier '8F' 2-8-0s during BR days, with a handful of ex-MR '1F' tank engines and '2F' 0-6-0s for local shunting work. The LMSR Beyer-Garratts were occasional visitors from the Midlands, but none were allocated to the depot. Canklow's engines were transferred away in May 1965 and official closure took place on 11 October, but the shed remained available to service visiting steam locomotives until September 1966.

As mentioned previously, Neepsend sheds' origins reach far back into early MSLR days. Even in the 1880s the shed was very well equipped, having shops for painters, joiners, coppersmiths,

fitters and spring work. One curious little establishment was the 'stick hole', a small outbuilding near the turntable whose purpose has not yet come to light! Closure took place when the new steam/electric depot at Darnall was made ready during 1943, albeit without any electric locos being available. The 10-road steamshed could hold 60 locomotives, and the 70ft turntable could accommodate the largest LNER locomotive likely to use the shed. Four roads were provided in

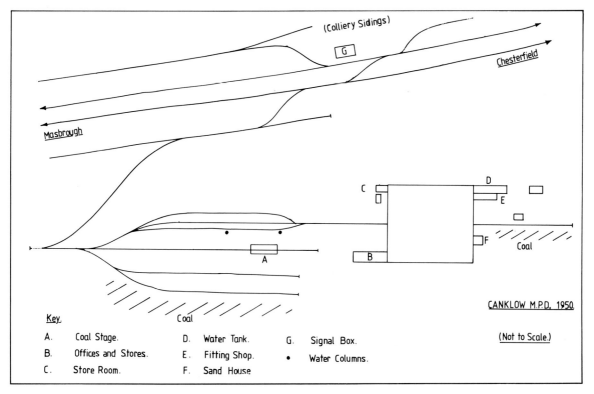

Key.

A.	Coal Stage.	D.	Water Tank.	G.	Signal Box.
B.	Offices and Stores.	E.	Fitting Shop.	•	Water Columns.
C.	Store Room.	F.	Sand House		

CANKLOW M.P.D. 1950.

(Not to Scale.)

Coal

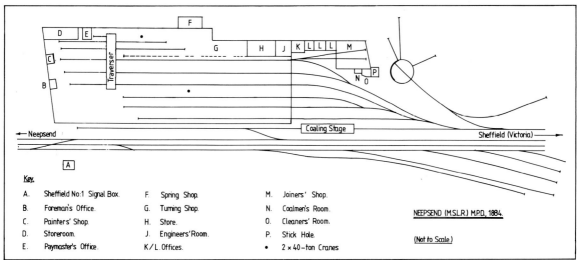

Key.

A.	Sheffield No:1 Signal Box.	F.	Spring Shop.	M.	Joiners' Shop.
B.	Foreman's Office.	G.	Turning Shop.	N.	Coalmen's Room.
C.	Painters' Shop.	H.	Store.	O.	Cleaners' Room.
D.	Storeroom.	J.	Engineers' Room.	P.	Stick Hole.
E.	Paymaster's Office.	K/L.	Offices.	•	2 × 40-ton Cranes

NEEPSEND (M.S.L.R.) M.P.D., 1884.

(Not to Scale.)

the electric shed, but this was not completed until 1952 and saw only eight years' service to the 1,500V locos, as in 1960 the depot was turned over to servicing the first arrivals of Sheffield's main line diesel fleet. Official closure took place on 17 June 1963, but after Tinsley diesel depot was opened the entire site was turned over to wagon repairing activities from May 1964. This activity still takes place today, but the depot is roofless and the coaling plant, water tower, turntable and other steam-age accoutrements have been removed.

Darnall played host to several life-expired veterans during the early years of nationalisation. The ex-GCR 'B7' 4-6-0s were able to manage up to 35 wagons on a slow goods, but the 'B8s' transferred from Annesley could only manage local trips between successions of repairs. One or two 'B7s' actually carried BR numbers, but all these, together with the 'Glenalmond' class 'B8s', dis-

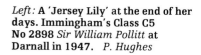

appeared by 1949. The little ex-MSLR Class N4 0-6-2T locos were still assisting trains from Rotherham up to Victoria, whilst empty coaching stock (ECS) workings up to Oughtybridge could often see one blasting uphill at 25mph with 14 bogies in tow. All had gone by 1955, leaving station pilot duties to the larger 'N5' class of 1891 vintage. Local trips to Rotherham, Doncaster, Barnsley and Penistone were handled by Class C13 4-4-2T locos until 1952, when 'J39' 0-6-0s and 'B1' 4-6-0s became available, but No 67424 returned in a blaze of glory on 27 May 1955. Working out to Doncaster on the 06.20 semi-fast, she returned on the 20.47 evening train with no

less than 11 coaches behind the bunker and running on time!

The 'B1' 4-6-0s took over nearly all ex-GCR line workings and soon reached York, Bradford, Banbury and King's Cross. But long after they had cleared the ground for themselves there occurred a most remarkable 'Indian Summer' amongst one class of locomotive long associated with Sheffield — the 'D11/1' 'Large Director' 4-4-0s. In the early 1950s all 11 of the class were employed on stopping trains such as the Doncaster and Penistone services and on the former CLC lines around Manchester. Five were based at Lincoln — Nos 62660, 3, 6, 7 and 70 — and these transferred to

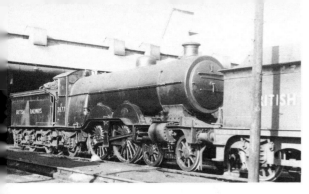

Top: **Former GNR Atlantic Class C1 No E2877.**
P. Hughes

Above: **New 'B1' 4-6-0 No 1181, resplendent in green
livery.** *P. Hughes*

Below: **A 'Pom-Pom' — 'J11' No 64325 in early BR
livery.** *P. Hughes*

Bottom: **'D11/1' 4-4-0 No 62662** *Prince of Wales* **at
Darnall.** *P. Hughes*

Darnall for the summer timetable of 1957 to work
ECS trains and locals to Nottingham or Lincoln.
Nos 62660 and 62666 reached York on Bridling-
ton trains when 'B1s' were in short supply.
Further work followed in the next summer, after
the engines had spent a winter in store at Darnall
and marked for scrap. During the 1958/59 winter
Nos 62664, 8 and 70 were stored at Darnall and
Nos 62660, 1, 5, 6 and 9 at Staveley, and the
summer service again saw all the class in use.
(Nos 62667 and 62670 reached Cleethorpes
during July 1959.) Storage for the winter followed
yet again, but the class was living on borrowed
time. Large-scale dieselisation was rapidly
approaching, and the 1960 summer services were
the last to be worked by the 'Directors'. The
Nottingham locals provided the final jobs during
September, and Nos 62662, 4, 7 and 9 were
hauled away to Doncaster during October.

Standard Class 9F 2-10-0s first appeared in
February 1956 on occasional freights from Toton
into Rotherwood, and later the following year
they saw passenger employment on some Bristol-
Bradford expresses and on several holiday extras
to Blackpool. That these machines could handle
main line express passenger turns with great com-
petence is well known today, but in 1958 the
extent of these abilities was yet to be discovered.
Lack of express passenger locomotives during the
summer saw No 92164 pressed into service on the
down 'Master Cutler' from Leicester on 10 July,
and No 92011 hauled the 07.32 Leicester-
Manchester into Victoria on the 11th, before
returning on the up 'South Yorkshireman'. The
train was observed leaving Victoria with great
gusto, accelerating rapidly and then being heard
making a very loud passage of Woodburn Junction, nearly a mile away. But the best performance was given the following day, when
No 92164 brought the down 'Cutler' all the way
from Marylebone, roaring along from Leicester to
Nottingham in just under even time and reaching
86mph in the process. Further occasional passenger work was done by the '9Fs', including the
'Thames-Clyde Express', the York-Bristol and the
Newcastle-Cardiff, but the high-speed abilities of
these machines did not please those in Authority,
who promptly ordered that such exploits must
cease forthwith.

An interesting event took place in November
1957, when 'Merchant Navy' Pacific No 35017
Belgian Marine, diesel-electrics Nos 10000 and
10203, and the former gas turbine locomotive
No 10800 were assembled with Bo+Bo and Co-Co
electrics in the Sheffield area. Tests were carried

out between Wharncliffe Wood and Deepcar to investigate the effects of hammer-blow on the track by different locomotives at various speeds, and testing at up to 80mph took place. This research was done in connection with the future West Coast main line electrification, and the use of the Woodhead line as a test bed for future rolling stock was considered but not taken up.

When steam power had nearly vanished from the area, enthusiasts received a welcome boost given by two unexpected visits of Swindon machinery during 1964. Western Region locomotives normally worked to Leicester with cross-country trains, but on 12 March 'Hall' class 4-6-0 No 7912 *Little Linford Hall* had to work through due to a diesel failure. This was followed on 15 August by No 6858 *Woolston Grange* on the same train, but this time the locomotive re-profiled the edges of Victoria's platform coping stones. After a halt to rectify a troublesome injector the errant engine set off to batter and scrape its way to Huddersfield, leaving particularly evident scars at Denby Dale. Two weeks of confinement at Hillhouse shed followed, until someone worked out a more suitable route for the return to less hostile pastures.

Above: 'B1' 4-6-0 No 61142 passes Attercliffe Road station with an up excursion on 18 October 1958. The train is about to pass below the ex-GCR main line east of Victoria.
K. R. Pirt

Right: Preserved ex-Somerset & Dorset Joint Railway 2-8-0 No 13809 passes Wincobank with an enthusiasts' special on 2 May 1981.
J. S. Whiteley

Passenger and goods facilities were altered significantly in the 10 years after 1945. British Railways renamed the ex-LMSR Pond Street station Sheffield (City) in September 1950, but the corporation did not like the suffix and successfully requested BR to alter the title to Sheffield (Midland) from June 1951. Rotherham (Westgate), terminus of the old S&R line, closed on 6 October 1952 but the nearby Holmes station survived until 19 September 1955. Wincobank lost its passenger traffic on 2 April 1956 but the goods traffic lasted another 10 years. On the former GCR lines Tinsley closed to passengers on 29 October 1951, but the goods traffic lingered on until March 1957. Two routes to Barnsley along the Blackburn Valley could not be tolerated, and the former South Yorkshire Railway route from Aldam Junction closed to passengers from 7 December 1953. Meadow Hall & Wincobank had been renamed Meadow Hall on 18 June 1951, and retained its goods facilities until 12 July 1965, but the original connection from Meadow Hall to Blackburn Junction was not severed until August 1964. The remainder of the route to Victoria, from Tinsley to Woodburn Junction, lasted until 5 September 1966 when Rotherham (Central) was closed and the last remains of the passenger service disappeared. Wadsley Bridge closed on 15 June 1959, but still sees service today for football matches at Hillsborough. Broughton Lane station had closed during April 1956, but freight was still handled for several years afterwards. Colliery traffic dwindled away too — the Birley colliery branch from Woodhouse closed in 1950 and the connection to Tinsley Park was ended on 1 March 1958. Local passenger traffic along the 'Old Road' was removed during the early 1950s, with closures at Treeton (29 October 1951), Woodhouse Mill (21 September 1953) and Holmes station on the former S&R on 19 September 1955. Shortly before this last closure the south curve at Masbrough, from Holmes Junction to Masbrough South Junction, was taken out of service on 5 July 1954 and was used by goods traffic only from then on.

Right: **Darnall's last surviving 'C13' 4-4-2T No 67439 takes a breather between station pilot duties on 27 September 1958.** *K. R. Pirt*

Above: **A four-car DMU reaches Woodburn Junction after travelling over the freight-only line from Rotherham with a football excursion train from Leeds to Sheffield in September 1982. The single-line flyover to Darnall MPD can be clearly seen in the background.** *S. R. Batty*

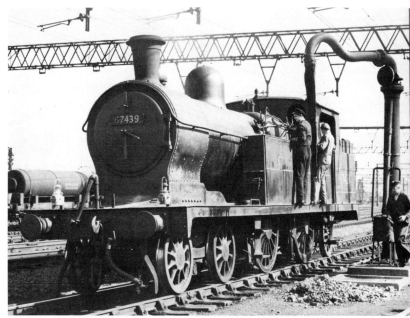

Above: A Stephenson Locomotive Society/Manchester Locomotive Society Hull & Barnsley railtour pauses at Midland station on 24 August 1952, headed by the last surviving Johnson Class 3 4-4-0, No 40726. *J. F. Henton*

Left: The 13.30 Barnsley (Court House)-Sheffield (Midland) arrives behind Ivatt '2MT' 2-6-2T No 41209. The locomotive is alongside the Sheffield 'B' signalbox, below the remains of the overall roof. *B. Morrison*

Below: One of the Western Region's green-liveried Standard Class 5 4-6-0s, No 73031, awaits departure from Midland station with the 16.45 Bradford (Forster Square)-Bristol express. *T. G. Hepburn*

Main line passenger services were gradually restored, but the job was made difficult by fuel shortages and maintenance backlogs. The Bristol-Newcastle trains and several St Pancras services were replaced in 1948, but a coal shortage in 1951 resulted in more cuts being made. Former GCR line trains took the brunt of these reductions, with the York-Bournemouth trains disappearing from December until May 1952. (The 'South Yorkshireman' was also affected, as mentioned previously.) During 1951 the best time to Marylebone was 3hr 45min, with five trains giving an average of 4hr 2min — a far cry from the days of 1905 when 10 up and 11 down trains averaged 3hr 35min and 3hr 25min respectively, admittedly often with lightweight trains of only four vehicles. The Midland main line service was similarly hamstrung, with the best time to St Pancras on the winter 1951/52 timetable only equalling the best St Pancras-Leeds time of 1905. First of all the main line services to regain prewar standards was the King's Cross-Victoria line. In the winter of 1953/54 the prewar 'Bradford Flyer', the 07.50 from King's Cross, was reinstated. By means of a connection at Retford the journey was brought down to 3hr 10min, by far the best available time to the capital. This was one of the first straws in the wind to suggest that the ex-GCR route was to be abandoned in favour of the ECML, but looking westwards to Manchester great improvements could be seen after completion of the electrification. From the winter of 1954/55 the 18.40 from London Road had 35min carved off its journey time, whilst 15 others (including the 'Continental') were speeded up by 10-23min, and the remainder had 2-5min reductions made. Fourteen trains completed the journey in 57-60min including stops at Guide Bridge and Penistone. Reductions of 2-5min were made again during the summer of 1956, bringing the fastest time across Woodhead down to 47min.

Diesel multiple-units began to appear at Sheffield from the winter of 1957/58 on the Victoria-Lincoln and Boston service, and also sporadically on the Hull (Paragon)-Midland trains during March 1958. The first regular down workings from Midland station began on 5 January 1959, when the York trains were handed over from a regular steam roster. Recovery on the main line proper began during the summer of 1954, when the 19.10 from St Pancras was accelerated by 28min to give a time of 3hr 22min to Midland station. The following two years saw the time whittled down to 3hr 10min, with a standard departure time of 15min past the hour

being introduced at St Pancras from summer 1957.

Management of the area's railways underwent a great change during 1958. After nationalisation the LMR had taken commercial responsibility for all areas west of Hazelhead and south of Heath, Chesterfield, but the operating and motive power functions belonged to the ER. The LMR looked after matters on its own main line and Grimesthorpe and Millhouses MPDs, but the coal and steel traffic of the area was entrusted to the Eastern Region's commercial organisation. From 1 February 1958 the ER took over completely, including the ex-LMR motive power depots and the main line from Chesterfield to Darton, near near Barnsley. The whole became the Sheffield District of Eastern Region, controlling MPDs at Darnall, Grimesthorpe, Millhouses, Canklow, Barrow Hill, Mexborough, Barnsley, Langwith Junction, Staveley and Tuxford. Such a change presented the first opportunity to completely overhaul the area's railway system and eliminate much duplication of effort. Consequently, a modernisation plan was drawn up which would replace the multitude of MPDs and goods yards with just one MPD, one freight terminal and one marshalling yard, and which would also eliminate steam power.

Finding the right locations for these establishments was difficult, but the little-used District Railway provided most of the answers. Despite the vast earthworks required (very much as had been needed 60 years beforehand), the line would be able to accommodate a new marshalling yard and MPD due to the availability of land along the line, and new entry/exit connections could be laid in quite cheaply to connect with the former LMSR/LNER lines. Grimesthorpe MPD site was chosen to house the new freight terminal, and any wagon repairs would be done at a new repair shop at Woodhouse Mill. After the £11million scheme was approved in early 1961, work went ahead quickly.

The goods depots across the city thus entered upon the last few years of their lives, and a glance at the quantity and variety of traffic handled during earlier BR days is of interest. Attercliffe handled mainly timber, and during April 1951 dealt with 8,530ton of material. (This yard continued to reflect LDECR history even at this late stage, when the shunting was carried out during 07.00-22.00 by a locomotive from Tuxford which arrived on a goods working at 06.55 and departed for home at 22.20.) Blast Lane, off the GCR east of Victoria, handled 2,350ton of coal traffic, whilst

Top: The 'Devonian' drifts past Pond Street goods yard behind 'Jubilee' 4-6-0 No 45699 *Galatea* on 18 June 1955.   *D. J. Beaver*

Above: Canklow 'B1' No 61093 departs from Midland with the 17.33 for Cudworth on 1 July 1963. *G. T. Robinson*

Left: Class 5 4-6-0 No 44888 awaits departure with the 17.20 for Manchester (Piccadilly) on a wet, dark evening.   *L. A. Nixon*

Right: The 16.10 Leeds (City)- Sheffield (Midland) leaves Rotherham Masbrough behind Class 5 4-6-0 No 44662 on 12 July 1963.   *D. P. Leckonby*

neighbouring Park goods moved a further 1,534ton. Perishables passed through Bridgehouses, Blast Lane and Wharf Street, and general traffic was dealt with at Queens Road, West Tinsley and Wicker. Sundries traffic for the month amounted to 9,512ton at Bridgehouses, 9,614ton at Queens Road and almost 11,000ton at Wicker. Queens Road had regular loadings to Ancoats, Bristol, Derby, Lawley Street, Leicester and Somerstown, but only one shift was worked to deal with off loading, sweeping and reloading. Queens Road was the parent depot to Wharf Street, the ex-LNWR depot, which was termed a 'spasmodic' depot without any regular traffic and was therefore staffed only on a daily basis. The hydraulic lift remained in use for lowering cartage and warehouse traffic to the lower yard, but the small MPD provided by the LNWR along the branch from Woodburn fell out of use by 1928. It remained standing as a derelict ruin for a further 40 years. Pond Street dealt with full wagonloads for collection only, and some yard space was made available for car parking. Bridgehouses, Wharf Street and Wicker had large areas let off as fixed space tenancies, clients of the latter two being Cadburys, Fyffes' Bananas, Allied Newspapers, Sheffield & Ecclesall Co-operative Society, Batchelors Foods, Gerrards Industries and Newton Chambers Ltd.

By the summer of 1963 the approaches of Tinsley yard were taking shape. A new north curve at Treeton was complete, and earthworks were finished off for the new outlets at the north-west end on to the former GCR line. The Catcliffe Tunnel and cuttings were opened out, and tracks were being laid in the 25-siding secondary yard. Steelwork for the new Tinsley MPD, amidst the heart of the yard, was being erected. As the scheme progressed, certain alterations and further developments were incorporated. Woodhouse Mill wagon repair shop was deleted, and such work was to be transferred to the former MPD at Darnall. To avoid changeover of diesel/electric locomotives, the 1,500V dc system was extended into the reception lines and express freight yard, and the new overhead equipment was insulated to enable a quick conversion to 6.25kV ac or even 25kV ac if this should ever be needed. For passenger services a new, improved Nunnery connection was planned to allow the concentration of all traffic at Midland and the complete closure of Victoria. The clearance of the old goods yard and colliery lines would allow a much-improved double-track connection to be laid in.

Since the boundary changes in 1958 had taken place, availability of diesel power and the spending of capital on the permanent way had improved passenger services enormously. Main line diesel power began to arrive in quantity during 1961, when Brush Type 2 (Class 31) locomotives were initially allocated to Darnall. In August 1960 the midday Pullman was chosen as a trial working for these machines, and very capable they proved themselves. These Pullmans and the 'Master Cutler' were soon averaging 60mph and the uprated 1,600hp and 2,000hp versions gave some truly dazzling runs to King's Cross over the following two years. (The prototype 2,800hp Brush *Falcon* worked on these trains for six months before going on to freight work in the east Midlands.) Sheffield's fastest time so far to London was revived in the summer of 1961, when the new 'Deltics' took over the 07.50 King's Cross-Bradford, now titled the 'West Riding'. The Retford connection gave a Sheffield arrival after

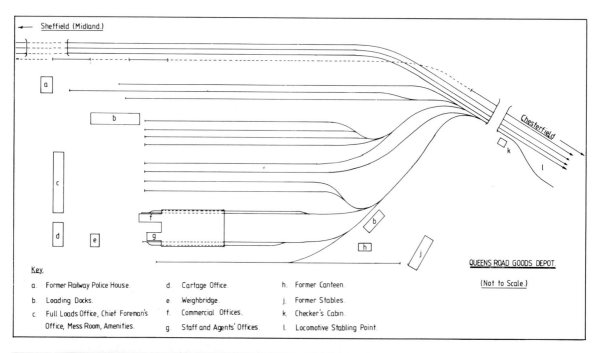

← Sheffield (Midland.)

Chesterfield

QUEENS ROAD GOODS DEPOT.

(Not to Scale.)

Key.

a. Former Railway Police House.
b. Loading Docks.
c. Full Loads Office, Chief Foreman's Office, Mess Room, Amenities.
d. Cartage Office.
e. Weighbridge.
f. Commercial Offices.
g. Staff and Agents' Offices.
h. Former Canteen.
j. Former Stables.
k. Checker's Cabin.
l. Locomotive Stabling Point.

Above: **Queens Road, goods depot.**
S. R. Batty/P. C. H. Robinson

Left: **The arches below Bridgehouses goods depot were used as warehouse space by several local establishments. These scenes taken in the 1950s show the storage and handling of various oils taking place.** *BR Western Region*

Above right: **Bridgehouses goods depot, 1950.**
S. R. Batty/P. C. H. Robinson

Right: **Wicker goods depot, 1950.**
S. R. Batty/P. C. H. Robinson

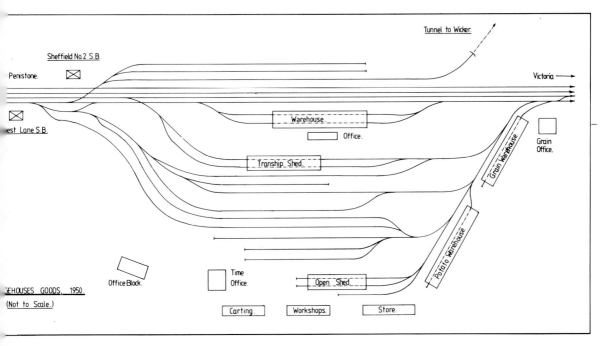

Sheffield No.2 S.B.

Penistone.

Tunnel to Wicker.

Victoria →

Warehouse.

Office.

Tranship Shed.

Grain Warehouse

Grain Office.

est Lane S.B.

Potato Warehouse

Office Block.

Time Office.

Open Shed.

GEHOUSES GOODS, 1950.
(Not to Scale.)

Carting. Workshops. Store.

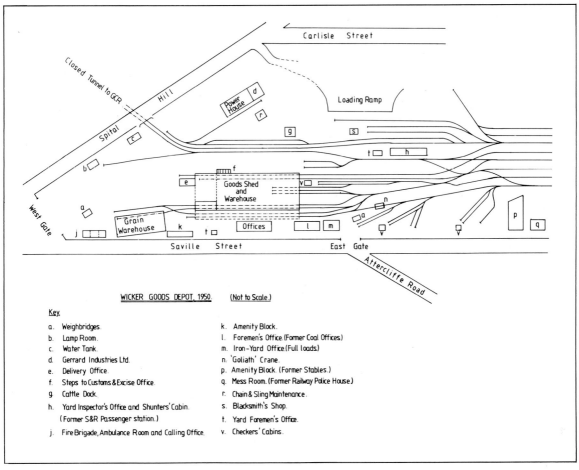

Carlisle Street

Closed Tunnel to GCR

Spital Hill

Loading Ramp

Power House d

r

c

g s

t h

b

f

e Goods Shed and Warehouse v

West Gate

a

n

p

j Grain Warehouse k t Offices l m a v q

Saville Street East Gate

Attercliffe Road

WICKER GOODS DEPOT, 1950.   (Not to Scale.)

Key.

a. Weighbridges.
b. Lamp Room.
c. Water Tank.
d. Gerrard Industries Ltd.
e. Delivery Office.
f. Steps to Customs & Excise Office.
g. Cattle Dock.
h. Yard Inspector's Office and Shunters' Cabin.
   (Former S&R Passenger station.)
j. Fire Brigade, Ambulance Room and Calling Office.

k. Amenity Block.
l. Foremen's Office. (Former Coal Offices.)
m. Iron-Yard Office. (Full loads.)
n. 'Goliath' Crane.
p. Amenity Block. (Former Stables.)
q. Mess Room. (Former Railway Police House.)
r. Chain & Sling Maintenance.
s. Blacksmith's Shop.
t. Yard Foremen's Office.
v. Checkers' Cabins.

2hr 50min, but this was short-lived as the 'West Riding' Retford stop was soon deleted. Glory returned in September 1963, when the Pullmans were taken over by the new English Electric Type 3 (Class 37) locomotives and reached King's Cross in a best-ever 2hr 40min. For a brief period from September 1962 the Midland line had offered the best London service, when the down 'Thames-Clyde Express' was accelerated to reach Midland in 2hr 57min.

But whilst these routes were thriving, Sheffield's other arterial route was entering its death throes. The former Great Central line's daytime passenger services from Marylebone to beyond Nottingham were axed from 4 January 1960, with new DMU workings filling in the gaps beyond there. Complete closure was not publicly mentioned yet, and the line was thought to be useful for diversions during the forthcoming electrification of the West Coast main line. A great deal of important long-distance freight traffic used the GCR main line, and Darnall Junction was passing much Class C and D traffic at this time. Principal trains were the 01.50 Woodford-Sheffield, 07.40 Woodford-York, 17.45 and 18.37

Below: **Wharf Street goods depot in 1959, with excursion notices for Scarborough (61p) and Southport (59p).** *J. H. Turner*

Woodford-York (Dringhouses), 15.50 (MFO) Park Royal-York (Dringhouses), 21.00 Marylebone-York and 23.59 Woodford-Hull. Up trains included the 21.40 Dringhouses-Marylebone, 03.10 Dringhouses-Woodford, 03.55 York (Skelton)-Banbury, 05.20 Dringhouses-Cardiff, 05.40 Dringhouses-Bristol, 10.25 Dringhouses-Annesley, 14.15 (TThO) Newcastle-Park Royal and 20.20 York-Banbury. The 05.20 Cardiff (the 'Welshman' in NER parlance) and 05.40 'Bristol' were pathed very close together throughout the run to WR territory. Locomotives, usually 'V2' 2-6-2s or 'K3' 2-6-0s, worked through from York to Woodford and made a water stop at Tinsley, amongst other calls en route. Steel traffic from Consett and Scunthorpe to South Wales amounted to three or four block trains daily, with two trains of unfinished products leaving Consett daily for Newport and Ebbw Vale. On the passenger front, the Newcastle-Bournemouth service survived during summer months only, a York-Banbury DMU taking over during winter. Working over Woodhead, the Manchester service was modified to give even-interval departures from Victoria at 45min past the hour from November 1960. The 'Continental' became diesel-powered throughout from November 1963, when English Electric Type 3 (Class 37) locomotives were given the first regular daytime diesel working over the route. However, Liverpool was cut from the train's schedule, leaving no through service from

Above: **Millhouses 'Jubilee' No 45590** *Travancore* forges up the 1 in 100 through Dore & Totley station with the 10.30 Bradford (Forster Square)-St Pancras on 3 October 1959. *M. Mensing*

Below: **A three-coach Derby stopping train behind 'Jubilee' 4-6-0 No 45675** *Hardy* leaves Dore & Totley on 22 August 1953. *P. Hughes*

Above: The Wicker entrance to Victoria in the late 1960s. Notice the advertised cheap return fares to London — day or weekend tickets for £2.37½ or £2.62½ respectively. *Sheffield City Library*

Below: Brush Type 2 No D5824 prepares to leave with the 09.28 Victoria-Cleethorpes on 16 August 1969. *V. Bamford*

Sheffield during the working day. This was rectified the following summer by a connecting service from Manchester (Piccadilly) to Liverpool (Central).

Services to Barnsley and Leeds were rationalised at this time by virtue of a new link at Barnsley (Quarry Junction) between the former SYR and MR lines. This allowed combination of the Leeds-Normanton-Wakefield-Barnsley service with the local trains from Midland into a single Sheffield-Barnsley-Leeds run, which took place when an hourly service from 09.30 to 21.30 was introduced from 19 April 1960. (Withdrawal of the remaining stopping trains to Leeds via Cudworth took place in 1967.)

Steam traction continued to appear at Sheffield, usually on through workings from the NER. Bitter weather during the winter of 1962/63 led to a shortage of diesel power and the use of York 'V2s' on the Newcastle-Bristol trains on several occasions. Even during the summer of 1964 a York 'A1' Pacific was entrusted with the 08.15 Sheffield-York on seven days in June and July. Home-based passenger work for Sheffield steam power was limited to a few trips along the Hope Valley on local stopping trains, usually with a Darnall or Canklow 'B1' or Standard 2-6-0 in charge.

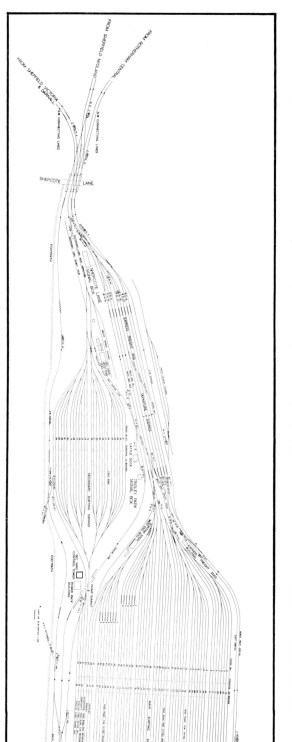

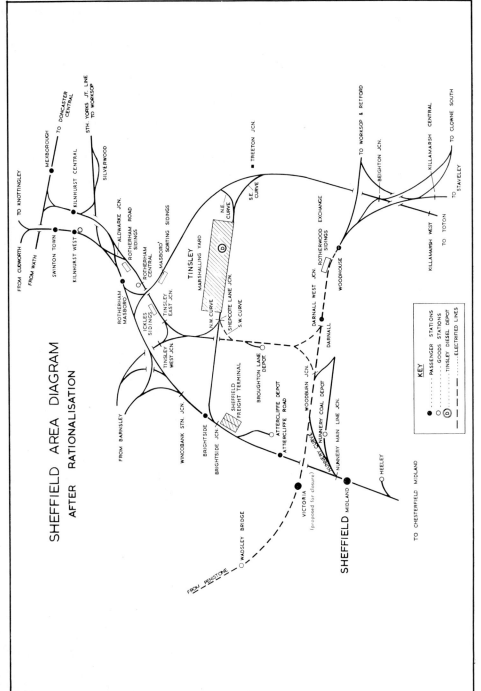

SHEFFIELD AREA DIAGRAM
AFTER RATIONALISATION

KEY
PASSENGER STATIONS
GOODS STATIONS
TINSLEY DIESEL DEPOT
ELECTRIFIED LINES

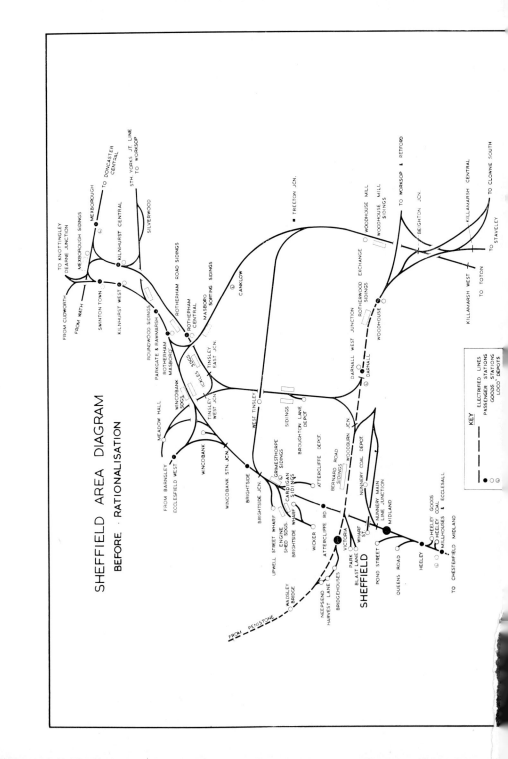

SHEFFIELD AREA DIAGRAM
BEFORE · RATIONALISATION

KEY
ELECTRIFIED LINES
PASSENGER STATIONS
GOODS STATIONS
LOCO DEPOTS

Left: **Part of the maintenance and workshop area of Tinsley diesel depot.** *BR*

Below: **A general view of the exterior of the maintenance depot in October 1965.** *BR*

Meanwhile, the modernisation scheme rolled ahead with the closure of Pond Street on 7 October 1961, Queens Road on 11 May 1963 and Park Goods during October 1963. Work started on the Grimesthorpe freight terminal during late 1963, and over 700ton of goods daily were expected to be handled by the new depot under the National Sundries Plan. The site of Pond Street goods depot was cleared for work to begin on a new Sheffield Division headquarters building, to be known as Sheaf House. Tinsley yard's last connection, at Shepcote Lane, was laid in during summer 1964, whilst the diesel depot had been opened on 24 February. This double-ended 12-track shed could support maintenance activities on 10 locomotives per shift. No cranes were provided, as engine lifting was not to be done at the depot. The total initial allocation of locomotives was 159, including 23 English

Electric Type 1s, 32 Brush Type 2s and 33 Brush Type 4s. Grimesthorpe freight terminal opened during summer 1965, and the remaining local depots at Blast Lane, West Tinsley, Wharf Street, Bridgehouses and Wicker all closed from 12 July. Wicker was gutted by fire just over one year afterwards on 31 July 1966, a sad end for Sheffield's first monument to the railway age.

Lord Beeching officially opened the entire £11million scheme on 29 October, by which time new Freightliner services were getting off the ground. Two trains left Tinsley daily for Stourbridge and Great Bridge, grossing up to 800ton. A new Freightliner terminal was built at Masbrough sidings and opened in July 1967 with a service to Glasgow. London was also served, by a 22.00 departure which returned from King's Cross at 02.55 after some pretty smart turnround work. This service was found to have spare capacity

Below: **Class 45 Nos 45.001 and 45.018 and Class 13 Nos 13.002 and 13.001 outside the maintenance depot in August 1979.** *G. Williams*

Right: **A tanker and a perishables van pass over the retarders on their way to separate destinations in the main yard.** *S. R. Batty*

amongst the open container flats, and so was used to run an extra working of steel from Sheffield to Cardiff from late 1967. Swansea was served by a working from the following spring.

A casualty of the new Freightliners was the 'Condor', a London (Hendon)-Glasgow (Gushetfaulds) nonstop container train which ceased to run as such from 26 October 1967. Started in March 1959, the service had carried over 70,000 containers and earned £1.5million, including revenue from the ex-Birmingham 'Condor' after January 1963. The train had used the NMR route ever since 1959, passing Masbrough during the night on its northward journey. Motive power was usually a pair of Metrovick Co-Bo Type 3 locomotives (single units were used when the train was lightly loaded), but other Type 2 diesels and steam power were used during non-availability of the regular fleet. This period saw

the final demise of steam power in Sheffield, with Canklow's allocation being dispersed during May 1965. By this time the remaining locos were in such a poor state that the locomotive men's union, ASLEF, complained to MPs about the near-derelict state of remaining steam power in the Sheffield, Chesterfield and Doncaster areas. Coming from railwaymen who had learnt to live amidst a 'make-do-and-mend' state of affairs over the past years, this was a pretty damning conviction of the local motive power scene. Ex-LNER 'B1' 4-6-0s survived on the Hope Valley locals, but these succumbed to the chatter of Type 2 diesel engines during October 1965 when Canklow was officially closed. Visiting steam power from the West Riding continued until September 1966, when all remaining steam servicing facilities were withdrawn.

Left: Crew change at Midland station, 3 September 1966. The summer Saturdays-only Bradford (Exchange)-Poole has arrived behind 'Jubilee' No 45562 *Alberta* in the charge of Farnley Junction men. The relief crew will take the locomotive on to Nottingham. *M. Stokes*

Above: Class 5 4-6-0 No 45073 heads for home with the 17.20 departure from Midland station for Manchester on 9 May 1966. *L. A. Nixon*

Left: Sheffield's scrapyards have dealt with vast quantities of redundant steam locomotives. A Stanier 2-6-0 is being broken up at T. W. Ward's yard at Beighton in February 1966. *L. A. Nixon*

5 1965-1983 — Modernisation and the Future

The year 1965 saw Midland station receive its first ever exterior clean-up in 95 years of operation, when the accumulated deposits were washed off during a largely nocturnal three-month operation. Perhaps someone had realised that a grimy station would not stand comparison with the almost completed Sheaf House, a glass, concrete, metal and plastic edifice which had risen on the site of Pond Street goods depot. Opened in the same year, this building housed some 500 staff who were transferred from various locations including the old Duke of Norfolk's house just east of the Chesterfield line. Line control offices at Rotherham (Westgate) and Victoria were closed down and the functions transferred to Sheaf House soon afterwards.

Services from St Pancras improved from 1966 when hourly departures for Sheffield (alternatively via Nottingham or Derby) were started, giving a standard arrival time at Midland of just past the hour. Eight trains continued farther north, four 'Scotches' and four to Leeds and Bradford. This period was the beginning of the transformation of the Northeast-Southwest (NESW) services, previously reliant to a large extent on the now defunct GCR cross-country routes. The WCML electrified lines would serve all traffic needs of Birmingham and Manchester from Euston, and St Pancras was selected to deal with all traffic along the Midland main line to Sheffield — but no farther. To this end the ECML service via Retford (by now down to 'Cutler' Pullman plus one other train) was to be forsaken. Despite the lack of trains travelling to King's Cross, the times were excellent — so much so that a Sheffield Airport proposal for internal flights was deemed to be a non-starter. All future London trains were to travel via the MR main line to Sheffield, where arrivals and departures would be closely related to a much improved NESW timetable. After the Retford connection with the 07.50 down from King's Cross was deleted, passengers instead had to leave St Pancras at the same time but reach Midland station 26min later than previously. The

torrent of protest was such that the train was accelerated to arrive only 4min later, a much more acceptable situation and, of course, not involving any changing. The 'Master Cutler' was transferred to the Midland line from October 1968, losing its Pullman cars and leaving Sheffield without any service to King's Cross. At the same time all trains on the line were slowed by 7-11min north of Nottingham due to a reappearance of the old enemy, subsidence, on the Erewash Valley route. Stopping trains to Derby and Nottingham were taken off, and the Hope Valley line only just survived the last of several attempts at closure which had been made since 1959. The stations at Heeley and Millhouses & Ecclesall closed during June 1968, leaving Dore & Totley as the only remaining station on the southbound climb out of the city.

After the bulk of the Modernisation Plan was completed in 1965, the largest fly in BR's ointment was Victoria. The new Nunnery curve provided a much better connection than the steep, narrow spur of 1870 vintage, even though reversal would still be necessary for Manchester-bound traffic when Victoria was eventually closed. During October 1965 a total of 24 trains per day were diverted to Midland station, these being on services to Doncaster, Hull, Lincoln, Grimsby, Cleethorpes and some to King's Cross, whilst the Manchester traffic, the 'Continental' and the cross-country runs to Swindon and Bournemouth remained at Victoria. But 1966 was a bad year, with the entire GCR main line disappearing from September (Rotherham Central closed to passengers from 5 September and to goods traffic in May 1968) and closure proposals being published for the Woodhead service in November. Suggestions to extend the 1,500V dc system into Midland station were dismissed as being too expensive, and Woodhead was seen as an ideal route for carrying heavy freight traffic only under the 1984 Trunk Route Plan. Consequently, the Manchester passenger service was diverted via the Hope Valley and the electrified

Left: **Midland station and the new Sheaf House in 1965.** *L. A. Nixon*

Below: **Class 47 No 1575 passes Sheffield South No 1 signalbox with a cement train from the Hope Valley on 5 July 1971.** *J. H. Cooper-Smith*

Bottom: **A Class 08 to the rescue. D3336 hauls a northbound train into the station after the train locomotive, Class 46 No 192, has been removed following a fire on board.** *L. A. Nixon*

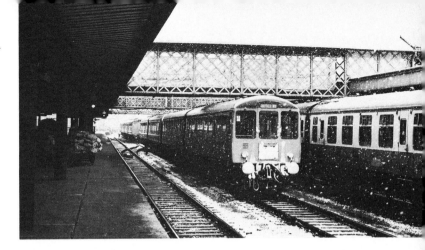

Right: Snow falls in Midland station, Christmas Eve 1970. *L. A. Nixon*

Below: Class 45 locomotives on Northeast-Southwest services; No 45.014 on the 09.40 Plymouth-Edinburgh meets No 45.053 on the 08.15 Plymouth-Leeds near Queens Road on 21 April 1979. *G. W. Morrison*

services ceased on 5 January 1970. A DMU service was retained on the Penistone and Huddersfield trains, but the line's major traffic now became a procession of coal, steel, chemicals and scrap hauled by Class 76 Bo+Bos, many of which were modified for working in multiple. The Class 77 Co-Co locomotives were quickly sold off to the Netherlands, where they are still performing well at the time of writing.

Over the 10 years after closure, Victoria continued to see many passenger trains diverted away from the Hope Valley to allow maintenance work to be carried out within the damp confines of Totley and Cowburn Tunnels. But the freight traffic came under a cloud with the declining economic situation, and by 1980 the line was handling only 40 trains daily out of the 120 which the route could accommodate.. No traffic was generated along the route, the MGR coalflow was rapidly dwindling, and furthermore the cost of renewing or replacing the electrical equipment was deemed to be prohibitive. (Conversion to 25kV ac would cost £44million.) BR made known its intention to close the line altogether, and a long and vociferous battle followed with railway unions and the local councils involved. Most of the freight traffic was diverted away, and the first route across the Pennines died quietly on the night of 24 July 1981. Victoria station had decayed to a windswept shell by this time, and was disturbed only by the Huddersfield DMUs on their way to or from reversal at Nunnery. Recently the South

Left: Class 20 locomotives Nos 20.194 and 20.171 take a mixed train past the reception sidings at Tinsley yard. *S. R. Batty*

Below left: Class 08 No 08.485 returns to Tinsley yard with a mixed bag of wagons on 3 March 1982. *S. R. Batty*

Below: An assortment of motive power in the traction maintenance depot yard, including a Class 55 'Deltic' from an enthusiasts' railtour. *J. S. Whiteley*

Right: Class 56 No 56.085 hauls empty MGR wagons along the de-electrified curve from Tinsley yard to Broughton Lane in March 1983. *S. R. Batty*

Below right: A pair of Class 76 locomotives, Nos 76.034 and 76.032, enter the closed Victoria station on 19 October 1979 with an MGR train of coal from Rotherwood to Fiddlers Ferry power station. *H. Taylor*

Yorkshire Passenger Transport Executive (PTE) has agreed to subsidise the diversion of these trains from Penistone (Barnsley Junction) to run via Barnsley and thence directly to Midland station for a trial period of 12 months, commencing in May 1983. Should this be successful, the former SA&MR line will be closed and lifted from Deepcar to Dinting, and Victoria station will be completely demolished after over 130 years of use.

Clearance of derelict sites took place steadily, and on occasions revealed interesting glimpses of the past. Bridgehouses and Rotherham (Central) were demolished during 1969, and Rotherham (Masbrough) was refurbished during 1970. At Masbrough, the platform gaslamps were replaced with fluorescent fittings recovered from Victoria station — an excellent example of recycling. Much of the Nunnery area network was razed to the ground and reclaimed in connection with a new road into Sheffield city centre, but the former LNWR three-level bridge survived until October

Above: **The desolate remains of Victoria station in 1982.** *S. R. Batty*

Left: **Semaphores at Masbrough. Nos 20.127 and 20.017 taking an up freight along the ex-NMR route on 21 September 1976.** *B. Morrison*

Above right: **The 18.10 departure for London (St Pancras) leaves Midland station behind Class 45 No 45.148 on 31 August 1980.** *G. W. Morrison*

Right: **Class 44 finale. Nos 44.005** *Cross Fell* **and 44.002** *Helvellyn* **pause with the 'Borderman' railtour on 24 July 1977.** *C. J. Tuffs*

1975 before demolition. The area overlooking Blast Lane and Park (Goods) has been re-profiled, grassed over and planted with trees to such effect that no trace of former activity remains. Park (Goods) was demolished during 1979, but the coal offices and some arches have been retained as part of the Canal Rehabilitation Scheme. The original S&R lines to Wicker have been turned into a long siding giving access to Firth Brown's steelworks, and the Wicker site was levelled during 1979 to make way for a car showroom.

During this reclamation the original carriage turntables of 1838 were uncovered in the yard. Today, the retaining wall below Spital Hill is all that remains of this railway terminus, with the blocked-off entrance of the tunnel overlooking the ranks of parked cars and giving the only clue to the site's hectic past.

The last civil engineering work in the area commenced during 1971, in connection with the first stage of the introduction of multiple-aspect signalling (MAS) to the area. During January, work

Left: A two-car DMU leaves Dore & Totley to call at all stations along the Hope Valley to New Mills. The Chesterfield line of 1870 can be seen on the left, curving towards Bradway Tunnel. *S. R. Batty*

Centre left: Class 40 No 40.022 labours towards Dore & Totley with the Harwich-Manchester (Piccadilly) train on 28 August 1982. *S. R. Batty*

Below: The 08.48 Manchester (Piccadilly)-Sheffield passes the site of Heeley carriage sidings on 1 July 1975. In the foreground can be seen the trackbed of the new lines laid in 1900 by C. J. Wills as part of the No 1 contract of the widening scheme. *L. A. Nixon*

Right: Bare signal posts testify to the redundancy of the 1900 dive-under in this view of Class 47 No 1989 passing Heeley on a down express from St Pancras on 28 June 1972. Only three days have elapsed since the revised layout was brought into use. *J. H. Cooper-Smith*

Centre right: During the later stages of work on completion of Stage I of the MAS scheme, Class 47 No 1587 approaches Sheffield (Midland) on the former up slow line with the 11.25 Poole-Newcastle on 31 March 1973. *G. T. Heavyside*

Below: A Manchester (Piccadilly)-Cleethorpes DMU passes a collection of vehicles at the Sheffield bus depot near Heeley on 20 March 1981. *G. W. Morrison*

started on the reduction of the quadruple track out to Dore & Totley to double track, leaving an up loop between Heeley and Millhouses and a down loop from Heeley in to Midland station. Some of the MAS was completed by January 1972, when a temporary panel at Dore & Totley was used to control movements between Beauchief, Totley (East) and Tapton Junction and also dispense with the boxes at Dore (West) and Dore (South). Nearer to Midland station, the 1900 dive-under which took the down fast line under the up and down slow lines was taken out of use from 25 June 1972, after the fast and slow lines had been slewed together at Millhouses. Sheffield power signalbox, at the south end of the station, was commissioned between 24.00 on Saturday 20 January 1973 and 06.00 on Monday 22 January, when all trains were diverted to Victoria, Dore & Totley or Brightside. (The Doncaster DMUs ran via Tinsley yard.) This new box replaced installations at Sheffield 'A' and 'B', Sheffield No 1 and No 2, Heeley station, Heeley carriage sidings, Millhouses and Queens Road. Temporary panels remained at Dore & Totley and Brightside, and the official completion of Stage I of the MAS scheme was announced in June, when these were finally taken out of service. (The redundant box at Brightside Junction became a PW staff mess room.) Trains arriving from or departing for the south used a much reduced track layout. Down trains approached along the down main (the old up slow line) or down loop (the old down slow), the latter starting south of the old Queens Road signalbox. The down main passed through the centre arch of the overbridge at the end of the station, which had previously accommodated a shunting neck. Up trains departed on the new up main, previously used as the up fast. Platforms 1-5 and 7 were signalled for reversible working, with 6 and 8 being used for up trains only.

Work under Stage II of the MAS scheme was completed on 14 January 1979, when Wincobank box was abolished. July of the same year saw the loss of signalboxes at Holmes, Canklow and the five locations at Masbrough. Three years later, on 16 May 1982, Beighton Junction box disappeared and work commenced at Treeton. After a great deal of realignment and other work, Treeton Junction and Treeton South boxes closed during October 1982, completing Stage II and converting all signalling on the former Midland lines to MAS.

Today's Midland line service to St Pancras is the result of several years of pressure from travellers who felt Sheffield had been deprived of a good service to London ever since the loss of the King's Cross trains. Until 1969 the 'Thames-Clyde Express' called at Midland between 15.47 and 15.51 on the up journey, and between 13.14 and 13.20 in the down direction. Corresponding times for the 'Waverley' were 17.51-55 and 12.06-10, until the train was cancelled during the 1969/70 timetable and the down 'Thames-Clyde' retired to take over the path of the down train. The up 'Waverley' was replaced by a Leeds-St Pancras train. The 'Thames-Clyde' lost its title during the 1975/76 timetable, and was cut during the following year to a St Pancras-Nottingham service. Through trains to Glasgow had dwindled to one train plus a sleeper each day, and these ceased during 1977 with the introduction of the Nottingham-Carlisle/Glasgow trains. Two trains ran daily to Leeds until 1976, and from 1978 these were reduced to one train only on Saturdays and Sundays, which were axed from 16 May 1982, so bringing a final end to St Pancras-Leeds workings.

Pressing for an improved London service, the city council suggested to BR that High Speed Train (HST) sets should be employed on the service right at the start of the HST era. But all available HST units were earmarked for the West of England and ECML services, and BR stated that Sheffield would be best served by an electrified Midland line using Advanced Passenger Train (APT) sets to complete the journey in an estimated 119min compared to the 137min estimated for HST units. But the pressure was applied and maintained, and eventually BR agreed to a trial HST run to establish the practicalities of the idea. During the night of 20-21 March 1981 set No 254.004 performed a return run from St Pancras with a best time of 2hr 18½min. A service time of 2hr 22min, was seen as a practical target, but it was not to be so. The NESW 'Heart Line' HST service was about to be introduced, and would mop up any spare HST capacity for the immediate future. Thus Sheffield saw HSTs but not on their primary route. From 5 October 1981 18 HST sets took over the majority of NESW services from the Class 45, 46 and 47 power of nearly 20 years past.

Trains on the St Pancras service relied on Class 45/1 and 47/4 power but the HST cause was not lost yet. By a backhanded trick of fate, the recession which was killing off much of Sheffield's steel industry and BR's hopes of profitability suddenly came to the rescue. HST earnings on the Western Region and on the almost new 'Heart Line' service were not fulfilling expectations, and on the East Coast the solitary HST serving Middlesbrough

Above: **The 10.45 St Pancras-Sheffield (Midland) arrives behind Class 45 No 45.138 on 28 August 1982. The parked DMU sets have worked in from York and Huddersfield.** *S. R. Batty*

Right: **Down with the old, up with the new.** *S. R. Batty*

was cancelled. These three failings prompted BR to study an improved deployment of the entire 95-set fleet, and the Midland line was granted the use of sets pared off the reduced services. Six sets were transferred to the line from October 1982 (with the possibility of seven more from the following May), and from 4 October eight up and nine down trains went over to HST power. (A total of seven up trains and five down remained locomotive powered.) These HSTs are drawn from ECML stock, and each night finds one stabled at Neville Hill, Leeds and another at Bounds Green, London. The set running to and from Leeds is used to provide a local service for this leg of its journey, and restoration of a full St Pancras-Leeds service will be given due consideration by BR. The last locomotive-hauled run of the 'Master Cutler' took place on 1 October 1982, when the up train departed behind Class 45 No 45.137 *The Bedfordshire and Hertfordshire Regiment (TA)*. The train's locomotive headboard traditionally had only been carried on the single occasion during each year when the Master Cutler accompanied the train, and this was the last time that the headboard was ever to be carried, because HST sets have no means of affixing the board to the noses of the power cars.

South Yorkshire PTE produced a series of Land Use Transportation studies during the late 1970s to outline future possible developments within its area of responsibility. One feature of interest was

Above: **The HST era. A 7+2 set screams through Brightside on the 07.20 Penzance-Edinburgh on 4 September 1982.** *S. R. Batty*

Below: **A Leeds-bound DMU leaves Masbrough station and is passed by an HST set on the 07.30 Newcastle-Paignton service.** *S. R. Batty*

a proposal for a new station at Rotherham which would be sited on the ex-GCR line just north of the former Central station. This would be much more accessible than the rather remote Masbrough station, but a new connection from Holmes (known as the 'Rotherham Chord') would have to be installed. Finance seems to be the main stumbling block between BR and the PTE, and at present the latter has not proceeded beyond the discussion stage.

Electrification to St Pancras and of the NESW route both remain beyond the horizon, and the future availability of motive power and rolling stock must be equally as important as the availability of funds for investment. The present recession has hit Sheffield's railways and their customers very hard indeed, with freight traffic reduced drastically and Tinsley's secondary yard lying unused, but one only has to look at the city's railway history to see how past difficulties have been eventually overcome.

Right: **Track alterations and MAS work were almost complete at Treeton North when this view was taken in September 1982. Semaphore signalling here was the last to survive on the ex-MR lines in the Sheffield area.** *S. R. Batty*

Below: **Class 08 No 08.434 pauses between duties alongside T. W. Ward's works at Broughton Lane.** *S. R. Batty*

Appendix
Allocation of Locomotives

Neepsend (LNER) MPD Allocation, November 1935

Class B2 4-6-0: 5425, 5426, 5428
Class B6 4-6-0: 5052, 5053, 5416
Class B7: 5035, 5480, 5483
Class C1 4-4-2: 3273, 3276, 3287, 3299, 4412, 4420, 4428, 4434, 4449
Class C13 4-4-2T: 6059, 6061-4, 6066
Class D9 4-4-0: 5105-8, 5110 *King George V*, 5112, 6015, 6022, 6026, 6040-2
Class D10 4-4-0: 5431 *Edwin A. Beazley*, 5435 *Sir Clement Royds*
Class J10 0-6-0: 5643, 5670, 5677, 5723, 5725, 5792, 5798, 5823, 5838
Class J11 0-6-0: 5016, 5295, 5301, 5330, 5947, 5953, 5954, 5999, 6001, 6117, 6119
Class J39 0-6-0: 2782-4, 2947, 2948
Class N4 0-6-2T: 5513, 5602, 5605-7, 5611, 5617, 5620, 5625, 5629
Class 04 2-8-0: 5378, 5966, 6203, 6205, 6229, 6230, 6232-6, 6244, 6245, 6256, 6258, 6259, 6265, 6275, 6316, 6317, 6514, 6516
Total — 96

Sheffield (MR) Grimesthorpe, Ecclesall and Canklow Allocation, 1920

Class 1 2-4-0: 81-5, 87, 185, 186, 193, 232, 264, 265, 268, 270, 271
Class 1 4-4-0: 300, 303-6, 308, 317, 319, 320, 325-7
Class 2 4-4-0: 369, 373, 374, 376-94, 396, 412, 413
Class 1 0-6-0: 2410, 2473, 2487, 2502, 2503, 2636, 2642-4, 2646-50, 2652-6, 2658, 2659, 2662, 2667, 2717-21
Class 2 0-6-0: 2818, 2822, 2846, 2946, 2950, 2965, 2970, 3082, 3085, 3086, 3093-5, 3097, 3098, 3100, 3101, 3140-9
Class 3 0-6-0: 3325, 3343, 3471, 3475, 3476, 3480, 3482, 3485-7, 3499, 3568, 3631-4, 3636, 3637, 3639, 3660-9, 3705, 3749, 3752, 3754, 3755, 3758, 3798, 3819-21
Class 1 0-6-0T: 1639, 1694, 1755, 1796, 1855, 1857, 1861-3, 1866-9
Class 1 0-4-4T: 1232, 1250, 1255, 1256, 1258, 1392-6, 1398-1400
Total — 177

Sheffield (LMS) Grimesthorpe, Ecclesall and Canklow Allocation, August 1933

Class 4 4-4-0: 1005-8, 1032, 1047, 1056, 1063, 1076-9
Class 3 4-4-0: 730, 731, 733
Class 2 4-4-0: 351, 353, 362, 379, 381-3, 385, 387, 389, 394, 443, 487, 488, 534, 535, 600-2
Class 5P/4F 2-6-0: 13050, 13093-6, 13097, 13138
Class 4 2-6-4T: 2336, 2337
Class 2 0-6-0: 2944, 2950, 2965, 2970
Class 3 0-6-0: 3023, 3038, 3054, 3085, 3094, 3095, 3098, 3100, 3101, 3140-6, 3148, 3149, 3238, 3325, 3334, 3343, 3347, 3353-5, 3470, 3475, 3480, 3485, 3486, 3512, 3573, 3632, 3660-2, 3664-6, 3668, 3669, 3706, 3749, 3755, 3756, 3758
Class 4 0-6-0: 3919, 3980, 3981, 3982-6, 4174, 4197, 4200, 4242-6, 4407-11, 4421
Class 7 0-8-0: 9544, 9546-51
Class 3 0-6-0T: 16539, 16629, 16630, 16631, 16707
Class 1 0-6-0T: 1694, 1782, 1796, 1799, 1835, 1855, 1857, 1863, 1869, 1890-4
Class 1 0-4-4T: 1258, 1358, 1360, 1392-6, 1398, 1400, 1426
Total — 153

Sheffield (Grimesthorpe) Allocation, October 1957

Class 1F 0-6-0T: 41795, 41857
Class 6P5F 2-6-0: 42794, 42797, 42904

Class 4 2-6-0: 43115
Class 3F 0-6-0: 43243, 43254, 43332, 43335, 43388, 43637, 43669, 43715, 43731, 43745, 43749, 43800
Class 4F 0-6-0: 43844, 43872, 43882, 44039, 44087, 44174, 44212, 44265 44287, 44437, 44457, 44477, 44535, 44547, 44568, 44573
Class 5 4-6-0: 44802, 44858
Class 2 2-6-0: 46450, 46451
Class 3 0-6-0T: 47513, 47548, 47624, 47636
Class 8F 2-8-0: 48144, 48179, 48189, 48642, 48765
Class 2F 0-6-0: 58192, 58225
Total — 49

Sheffield (Millhouses) Allocation, October 1957

Class 3 2-6-2T: 40148
Class 4 4-4-0: 40907, 41190, 41199
Class 2 2-6-2T: 41209, 41245, 41246
Class 4 2-6-0: 43032
Class 5 4-6-0: 44661, 44830, 44847, 44986, 45056, 45297
Class 6P5F 'Jubilee' 4-6-0: 45570 *New Zealand*, 45576 *Bombay*, 45590 *Travancore*, 45594 *Bhopal*, 45600 *Bermuda*, 45607 *Fiji*, 45609 *Gilbert & Ellice Islands*, 45656 *Cochrane*, 45664 *Nelson*, 45683 *Hogue*, 45725 *Repulse*
Class 2 2-6-0: 46400, 46494
Standard Class 5 4-6-0: 73011, 73016, 73048, 73065, 73074
Standard Class 2 2-6-0: 78022-5
Total — 36

Canklow Allocation, October 1957

Class 1F 0-6-0T: 41835, 41875
Class 4 2-6-0: 43037
Class 3F 0-6-0: 43180, 43208, 43225, 43369, 43371, 43660, 43664, 43814
Class 4F 0-6-0: 44002, 44036, 44037, 44071, 44082, 44089, 44111, 44128, 44206, 44245, 44576
Class 5 4-6-0: 44944
Class 3F 0-6-0T: 47238, 47546, 47547
Class 8F 2-8-0: 48011, 48026, 48075, 48138, 48140, 48150, 48151, 48176, 48181, 48209, 48216, 48391, 48396, 48397, 48407, 48508, 48548, 48646
Class 2F 0-6-0: 58170, 58198, 58238
Class 2 2-6-0: 78026, 78027
Total — 49

Sheffield (LNER) Darnall Allocation, January 1947

Class V2 2-6-2: 845, 849, 881, 889
Class B1 4-6-0: 1063, 1066, 1087, 1088, 1108-11
Class B7 4-6-0: 1360-5, 1369, 1372, 1377-80, 1383-7, 1397
Class B17 4-6-0: 1647 *Helmingham Hall*, 1653 *Huddersfield Town*, 1657 *Doncaster Rovers*, 1662 *Manchester United*
Class D10 4-4-0: 2650 *Prince Henry*, 2651 *Purdon Viccars*, 2652 *Edwin A. Beazley*, 2654 *Walter Burgh Gair*, 2655 *The Earl of Kerry*, 2656 *Sir Clement Royds*, 2657 *Sir Berkeley Sheffield*, 2658 *Prince George*, 2659 *Worsley Taylor*
Class O1 2-8-0: 3579
Class O4 2-8-0: 3581, 3583, 3629, 3661, 3686, 3714, 3733, 3766, 3771, 3783, 3790, 3821, 3822, 3846, 3860, 3882
Class J3 0-6-0: 4134, 4141, 4144
Class J11 0-6-0: 4291, 4360, 4387, 4412, 4419, 4441, 4443, 4445, 4447
Class J39 0-6-0: 4753, 4808, 4809, 4878, 4890, 4960, 4973
Class C13 4-4-2T: 7404, 7406
Class Y3 0-4-0T: 8163, 8184
Class J62 0-6-0T: 8202
Class J50 0-6-0T: 8928, 8983, 8990
Class L1 2-6-4T: 9051, 9057, 9058, 9063
Class N4 0-6-2T: 9226-30, 9232-8, 9240-5, 9247
Total — 110

Sheffield (Darnall) Allocation, October 1957

Class B1 4-6-0: 61033 *Dibatag*, 61041, 61044, 61050, 61051, 61138, 61150, 61151, 61153, 61154, 61169, 61174, 61179, 61183, 61313, 61315, 61316, 61327, 61334
Class K2 2-6-0: 61724, 61728, 61747, 61760, 61761
Class K3 2-6-0: 61907, 61938, 61954, 61967
Class D11 4-4-0: 62660 *Butler-Henderson*, 62663 *Prince Albert*, 62666 *Zeebrugge*, 62667 *Somme*, 62670 *Marne*
Class O4 2-8-0: 63574, 63581, 63583, 63599, 63604, 63609, 63620, 63621, 63624, 63629, 63640, 63645, 63658, 63661, 63680, 63682, 63685, 63695, 63710, 63714, 63733, 63737, 63742, 63744, 63748, 63771, 63783, 63790, 63797, 63821, 63822, 63846, 63850, 63852, 63881, 63882, 63888, 63889
Class J11 0-6-0: 64329, 64373, 64387, 64394, 64419, 64441, 64443, 64445, 64447

Class J39 0-6-0: 64738, 64744, 64746, 64808, 64878
Class C13 4-4-2T: 67439
Class N5 0-6-2T: 69259, 69266, 69271, 69286, 69292, 69294-6, 69302, 69327
Total — 96

Sheffield (Tinsley) Allocation, October 1965

Brush Type 4 Co-Co: D1525, D1527, D1531, D1552, D1553, D1574, D1576, D1703, D1768-D1806, D1862-7, D1869-79, D1881, D1882, D1888, D1890-2, D1895-7

BR 0-6-0 Diesel Shunters: D3086, D3127, D3129, D3131, D3251-4, D3288, D3289, D3293, D3326, D3330, D3336, D3439, D3440, D3443, D3444, D3452, D3475, D3574, D3575, D3659, D3660-4, D3685, D3702, D3703, D3707, D3727, D4028, D4029, D4035-52, D4054-6, D4058, D4059, D4062-5, D4068, D4070-4, D4089-94, D4500-2

D4500-4502 were 'Master & Slave' units coupled for working the hump yard at Tinsley. The units were made up as follows:
D4500: Master D4188, Slave D3698
D4501: Master D4189, Slave D4190
D4502: Master D3697, Slave D4187

Brush Type 2 A1A-A1A: D5528, D5533, D5536, D5538-43, D5546, D5549, D5550, D5552, D5555, D5557, D5558, D5561, D5565, D5567, D5568, D5579, D5583-6, D5665, D5670, D5677, D5680-4, D5686, D5687, D5691, D5804-6, D5840-50, D5855, D5856, D5858-62

English Electric Type 3 Co-Co: D6728, D6729, D6742-54, D6796-6818, D6965-8

BR Type 2 Bo-Bo: D7624-34

English Electric Type 1 Bo-Bo: D8058-69

Total — 272

Sheffield (Tinsley) Allocation, December 1982

Class 08: 08.022, 08.033, 08.208, 08.209, 08.219, 08.244, 08.335, 08.389, 08.492, 08.507, 08.510, 08,523, 08,543, 08.655, 08.678, 08.729, 08.749, 08.782, 08.866, 08.877-80

Class 13: 13.001, 13.003

Class 20: 20.001, 20.004, 20.005, 20.008-11, 20.015, 20.026, 20.032, 20.035, 20.053, 20.055-60, 20.064-6, 20.076, 20.105, 20.128, 20.131-3, 20.144, 20.145, 20.154, 20.208-10, 20.212

Class 31: 31.302, 31.308, 31.311, 31.315, 31.316, 31.327, 31.404, 31.406, 31.410, 31.411

Class 37: 37.013, 37.046, 37.077, 37.121, 37.122, 37.128, 37.130, 37.132, 37.136, 37.169, 37.174, 37.209, 37.215, 37.226, 37.228, 37.245, 37.246

Class 45: 45.006, 45.007, 45.009, 45.010, 45.012-7, 45.019, 45.020, 45.022, 45.026, 45.029, 45.038, 45.048, 45.062, 45.063

Class 47: 47.217, 47.278, 47.279, 47.307, 47.310, 47.316, 47.319, 47.371, 47.372, 47,374, 47.375

Class 56: 56.001-19, 56.083-91, 56.094-56.107, 56.112, 56.113

Total — 181